The Outbreak of Covid-19: A Medical Worker's Journal In the Heart Of Italy's Pandemic

Natalie Evans

ISBN: 978-0-9706651-4-0

DEDICATION

To the Frontline Workers:
The Doctors, Nurses, Medical Personnel, and vital Support Staff who put themselves in harm's way during acts of war, hurricanes, earthquakes, Cholera, Ebola and Covid-19, including my fellow Med Techs (Barb Rash and Richard Quimby),
who are my very brave friends

Table of Contents

ACKNOWLEDGMENTS

Special acknowledgements to my husband, Rick Evans, who always supports me in every venture I do and takes such good care of me. To my mother, Patricia West, and my mother-in-law, Betty Evans-Jordan, who both have exhibited great bravery! Thank you to nephew Richard Evans, who formatted the cover! To my children and their spouses, who I am immensely proud of: Nate & Savana, Canaan & Taylor, Elijah and Alexandra. To my grandchildren & the ones yet unborn: Titus, Aiden, Nora and Graysen. I love you all. To my siblings, nieces and nephews, who I know have prayed for me. I can never offer acknowledgements without adding my father, Robert (Bob) West,
who passed away in 2002. You are forever missed and you have always paved the way for me, Dad. What a great cloud of witnesses we have!

Lastly, to my beautiful coworkers who have graciously given me permission to add their perspectives to this narrative.

Dr. Mark Agness
Katie Kunnen
Dr. Peter Kwan
Taylor Pitkin
Dr. Michael Post
Barb Rash
Dr. Bob Spencer
Shannon Wood

This is a personal narrative by Natalie Evans of her service in Cremona, Italy. Natalie wishes to thank Samaritan's Purse for the opportunity to serve on the Disaster Assistance Response Team and for the opportunity to share her account. This is a personal journal written by Natalie, as well as personal thoughts and contributions by Dr. Mark Agness, Katie Kunnen, Dr. Peter Kwan, Taylor Pitkin, Dr. Michael Post, Barb Rash, Dr. Bob Spencer, and Shannon Wood. Samaritan's Purse was not involved in the writing or editing of this book.

FORWARD

I asked my dear friend and coworker, Barb Rash, who has been a longtime Medical Laboratory Technologist, to share her thoughts about her time working in Italy during this virus. Barb is in her early 60s and works tirelessly. She has served in many different disasters all over the world. She suffered great loss when her preacher father passed away when she was 19. She married the love of her life, Herb, and adopted her two beautiful children from South Korea, who are in their twenties now. She has worked as a Medical Technologist for more than 40 years and served in the Ukraine, Central America, Ecuador, Iraq, Mozambique, Haiti, and most recently, Italy. She is a testimony to the fact that age is not a deterrent to serve! I love Barb and I count it a gift that she has shared a little of her heart here. Her words are much of how all of us felt. When we deployed to Italy, it was at the peak of the unknown and deadly virus, COVID-19.

Philippians 1:21 (NIV)

"For to me, to live is Christ and to die is gain."

Powerful words I have quoted many times. but it was in Cremona, Italy they became real to me. I can't help but ponder why now? I have seen death before.

Many times, throughout my career, I was called to the emergency room to collect blood from a patient who had been in an accident or suffered some other life threating event, and many died. In Ecuador I saw how an earthquake takes and shatters life in a few moments in time. In Iraq, I saw the unthinkable cruelty of war, manifested by children's lifeless, limbless bodies and their mother's unstoppable weeping for them. In

Mozambique I heard story after story of families watching as Cyclone Idai ripped their loved one away and the raging waters engulfed them.

Yet, in this first world country with all the modern conveniences of modern medicine, we are in the parking lot of the 600 bed Cremona Hospital, filled with patients who have the coronavirus. It has now been labeled a worldwide pandemic. Italy's healthcare system has been overwhelmed. The doctors and nurses of this hospital are now the patients, and they are dying. Once again Samaritans Purse has been asked to come serve in Jesus name through our Emergency Field Hospital. We arrived on March 17th, 2020 and witnessed a tent hospital come to life in hours.

Then the sick came. We filled beds with those whose very breath was dependent on the ventilators we provided.

I stood just outside the tent door and a voice whispered, "There is death inside those walls. People are dying. They are younger than you."

Then the word of God came. "For me to live is Christ and to die is gain." "Will I die, Lord?" I ask.

"Trust Me," He said.

I unzipped the door… and walked inside.

He is faithful.

Barb Rash, Medical Laboratory Technologist

1 MISSIONARY OR MISS AMERICA

Long ago, as a little girl, I was given a book by my parents titled *Tombi's Song*. It was a story of a little girl in Africa. My grandmother used to say, (and pardon the reference, but this is how grandmother's sometimes think), "You'll either be Miss America or a missionary to Africa someday." Now Miss America sounded glamourous, but a missionary not so! I had no interest whatsoever in becoming a missionary! The Lord later captured my heart and my love for Him grew! I grew up, married my awesome husband, had my four beautiful children, supported missionaries along the way, and as my kids grew, so did their faith. All of our children ended up doing missions throughout the world for a short time. Our oldest son spent time in Thailand and Costa Rica. Our second son spent time in Africa and India. Our third son did missions all over the Pacific West of America and our daughter spent some time in US missions. I was especially touched by a video done by our son, Canaan, after his trip to Africa. I was so emotionally moved. During that time, I had decided to go to school to focus on an occupation I could enjoy that would keep me busy as my children were soon to leave home and live their own lives. I became a Medical Laboratory Technologist. I had enjoyed homeschooling them for most of their childhood and now they were growing up. While in school, I was inspired to start a mission group called Mission:Hope, in hopes of taking groups on missions and inspiring change in their lives and in the lives of those we went to serve. Our one and only mission was to Sakwa, Africa to serve with Roberta Peterson of Hope Africa Ministries. It was a learning experience and certainly a life-changing one. I will always be grateful to Roberta for hosting our small team.

Not long after that, one of my dreams was to hike part of the Appalachian Trail. I have a great love for the outdoors! My husband gave his blessing and a few ladies and myself (all over fifty) planned a trip with Going the Distance ministries in Tampa, Florida to hike a portion of the A.T. It was a fantastic trip and also extremely difficult. As I hiked those beautiful mountains, with a forty-pound pack on my back, I wondered if I could finish. My heart was working extra hard and I prayed a lot during that trip. I recited scriptures that gave me courage during those days of hiking. I also resolved to memorize more scripture when I returned home, feeling my memory bank was deplete. When I returned home, I found Psalms 46 and decided to memorize that chapter. Over and over each night, I recited those words and hid them in my heart. One evening after working my regular job at a local laboratory, I came home feeling a bit despondent. I prayed, "Lord, I know you have something for me to do! Please show me what purpose I have now!" I went into our home office and typed three things to search on the internet: medical laboratory, missions, and job. Up popped a job description for something called, "Disaster Assistance Response Team, DART" with Samaritan's Purse (SP). I had heard of Samaritan's Purse, but this very much intrigued me. Inspired, without much thought at all, I decided to apply and did so right then and there (later I told my husband what I did, which his response was to be as intrigued and excited as I was!) To my great surprise later that week, I did get a call from a recruiter at Samaritan's Purse. After my interview, I was accepted as part of the DART team and I was so blessed to attend the very first DART training in Boone, North Carolina, with the first thirty-plus medical personnel to train! As with any training, they graciously gave us a certificate that stated we had completed the training…and at the bottom of the certificate was a verse. It was Psalms 46:1 (NIV), "God is our refuge and strength, an ever-present help in trouble," the very 1st verse of the scripture I had resolved to memorize! This is how God many times puts His fingerprint on the tapestry of our lives. I can never forget how He has led me and how His eyes have been on me and are on every person in mankind. For this season of my life, He had a directive for me and this small scripture gave me one extra dose of confidence that He had not forgotten me.

Being accepted into the DART team with Samaritan's Purse occurred in 2015. Soon after, an earthquake hit Ecuador and the DART team was deployed there to set up a field hospital in the area. That experience was life-changing for me and I will never forget the people and team I was blessed to serve with.

Since then, SP made themselves available to serve on many disasters, helping in Jesus' name. Family and work responsibilities made it so that I could not be a part of subsequent deployments. Though it pained me to not be able to go on certain deployments, I felt I could always trust that God would lead me when the timing was right.

This year around January 2020, a virus was discovered in Wuhan, China. We Americans felt far-removed from this though it was in the news. Random videos showed Chinese people passing out on the streets. However, it then hit Italy and word was out that the hospitals were overrun. It was then that Samaritan's Purse offered their help in the Lombardy region of Italy where the Coronavirus had hit the hardest. I had taken a week off from work to be with my grandchildren in Texas. On my last day with my grandkids, I texted my boss at the lab I was employed by in my hometown in Florida. She said the laboratory had closed its door that very day and everyone, including myself, had lost their job! I worked a part-time job, and wondered what God had next. I didn't have long to wait, as only 32 hours later, I received a text from SP. Was I available to go to Cremona, Italy for 4 weeks and how soon?

When you know God is calling you to something, your heart beats extra fast… and you almost can't stop long enough to think about it. You just know sometimes. It was hard to share this with my husband and entire family. Would they agree? How would they feel? Though my mother and siblings had a very hard time with this and other friends thought I was crazy, my husband (as a believer) also knew and trusted that God was leading me in this, even though it would be a sacrifice for him as well. Within four days of getting home from Texas, I was on a plane headed towards Italy.

This is simply a personal narrative of my experience as a Laboratory Technologist. Several of my coworkers (nurses and doctors) have graciously shared some of their experiences in this narrative as well, of which I am very grateful. The nurses and doctors in Italy and throughout the world are heroes to me. They put themselves on the frontlines of this disease; a disease that put fear into most of the whole world. They were the ones who, front and center, served those who had contracted COVID-19. They loved on them and suctioned out their lungs. They lovingly served them. They prayed silently for them. When this virus is someday eradicated, let it be known that this virus didn't have a cure during the frightful months that the world shut down. This virus would be known as the virus that stopped the world during our advanced culture. People lost their jobs. Restaurants shut down. Travel shut down. The stock market fell in dramatic proportions. This was a time of uncertainty that occurred in all of America and the entire world. It was a time that the majority of Americans faced fear.

The following are my personal journal entries during my time in Italy. It's not eloquent, but simply my thoughts during that timeframe that I pray will illuminate much of what many of us felt. Included are accounts from doctors and nurses, who served on the ground in Italy and New York City.

2 PREPARING FOR DEPLOYMENT

March 20, 2020

These are the most interesting times I and others have ever experienced in our lifetimes. I consider my mother, who is nearly 80 and my mother-in-law at 86 years old. Never in their lifetimes have they seen the world stop like this. Ever.

Restaurants are closing or scaling down their menus (so as to not waste food), retail stores are cutting back their hours and airlines are asking for help. Our 25-year-old son got a wonderful fulltime position with the YMCA in Lafayette, Colorado and he and his entire staff were laid off from their position effective March 23, 2020. We wonder how our other two adult sons will fare; one is a missionary with YWAM and the other works for the humanitarian group, Mercy Ships. Our daughter is a musician and her income has been severely cut.

And I lost my job exactly one week ago.

However, God's timing is no mistake. I have been an avid reader of first-person accounts of tragedies and survival stories my whole life. What I have noticed, beyond a shadow of a doubt, is that God is consistently faithful to those who call on Him.

Within 32 hours of losing my job, I was contacted by the Samaritan's Purse International Disaster Response Team (DART) of which I am a part of. Those of us on the team respond when needed and able. I was notified on a Sunday morning. I spoke to my husband that day to hear his thoughts and we made the decision that I was to go. The timing seemed to have God's fingerprint on it.

Much goes into preparation before leaving on a deployment. My deployment, this time, was to be 30 days plus a two-week quarantine. Taking care of bills, taxes, our widowed mothers' needs and packing for the trip ensued.

My typhoid immunization was overdue, so my first order of business was to get that shot scheduled. My husband and I drove south from our hometown two hours to the Passport Clinic in Boca Raton. Nurse Practitioner Karen Kluge was there to greet me.

"Where are you going?" she asked. With a slight hesitation, I answered "Italy." (Keeping in mind that Italy was considered the frontlines of this virus with over 400 deaths a day. They currently have a death-rate over 78.5% if you get the Coronavirus.) So, it's a very scary time in Italy. Most people would think you were completely crazy to head that way.

Karen asked, "Who are you going with?" I said a humanitarian group called "Samaritan's Purse," to which she smiled and replied, "Franklin Graham?" "Are you a believer!?" I asked. She said, "Yes, I am and we're praying right after I give you this shot!"

I had my first God-appointment before I even got out of town!

Before I left, I saw a video post by Ken Isaacs (VP of Programs and Government Relations with Samaritan's Purse) with the Cremona (Italy) hospital's Italian Director, singing "Take Me Home, Country Roads." As I listened to that, tears came to my eyes. No one could know that I felt God was comforting me again about this deployment. Every night when I was a little girl, moving from my beloved West Virginia mountains to Florida, I sang myself to sleep with that song. I felt God put that song out there just for me.

So, finally, today has come, and though my body is a bit tense from preparations, I am on my way via Palm Beach International airport to Charlotte, North Carolina and then onwards to Greensboro, NC.

Tomorrow, as God wills, I will be on the Samaritan Purse DC8 with others, as we head to Milan, Italy into the heart of the Coronavirus.

"Lord, I am no ordinary fool. I am a fool for You. You direct my paths. You lift up and lay low. You have taken the best and the brightest who love You, home to heaven, sometimes before it seemed right or ready for them to go. I know Your hand is with me, no matter the cost."

Well, I made it to Palm Beach International and funny story. In an effort to stay healthy, I packed protein powder and green powder. My suitcase didn't get very far, before I got the full "drug" pat-down at the airport and, alas, all my protein and green powder was taken away. I should have known better! At least I still have my supplements. Keep trusting in God's care, Natalie!

Post deployment thoughts: As I read through my own journal and the thoughts of others, I am more fully aware how God has prepared the way for us to deploy. There is also no doubt adrenaline plays a role in getting us to our destination. That adrenaline seems to remain in the first few weeks of a new situation! I believe it is God's way to help carry us through difficult and stressful situations!

A Nurse's Perspective (Taylor Pitkin):

Taylor was born and reared in Huntington, WV and obtained her degree in nursing from her hometown's Marshall University. She is second in birth order of four, with two sisters and a brother. She spent 9 months serving with World Medical Mission at Hospital of Hope in Togo, Africa from October 2018 to June of 2019. Towards the end of her time there, she was interviewed to work with Samaritan's Purse International Disaster Response Team and deployed with the team to the Bahamas after Hurricane Dorian and to Italy in response to the COVID-19 pandemic. She recently moved to Knoxville, TN to accept a job at the University of Tennessee Medical Center where she works as a labor and delivery and medical ICU nurse, and has the support of her hospital to continue serving with DART.

It was the weekend of March 14th and I remember thinking to myself, "I should pack my bag." Coronavirus was just starting to shut down the city, and I had this feeling that maybe I should be ready. Not long after, Samaritan's Purse sent out an alert that they were deploying the emergency field hospital to Italy as a respiratory support unit. My heart beat wildly as I entered my availability and the next day, I received the call to leave. Unlike the anxiousness I felt when I was first called to respond to Hurricane Dorian a few months ago, this time a mixture of adrenaline and excitement guided my preparations. Those feelings affirmed that the Lord was calling me exactly where He wanted me.

We landed on the ground with the first wave of the hospital on March 17th and were welcomed by sheer gratitude—that's one thing that will always stick with me from this particular response. Though not there to be served, the Italians found ways to do just that: our accommodations, the aid of their Air Force in setting up the hospital, and so much food and chocolate throughout the month you cannot even imagine it! We were told, "Your team is an answer to our prayers. In the wake of multiple cities being overwhelmed, Cremona was being overlooked."

A Nurse's Perspective (Shannon Wood):

I grew up in Wisconsin with my family of 7. I went to Pensacola Christian College in Florida and graduated with my Bachelor of Science in Nursing in 2016. From there, I started as an ICU nurse at Sacred Heart Hospital in Pensacola and continued working there until this year. Now I am pursuing my dream of disaster relief medical missions (through DART) and other medical mission opportunities. Since I joined DART in 2018, I've deployed to the US/Mexico Border, the Bahamas, Iraq, and now Italy.

Since I was a little kid, I've always had a passion for helping people when they need it most, but it's taken me step by step through life to figure out what that looks like and how I can do that best. First, I figured out that I wanted to help people in medicine. I later figured out that I wanted to do that in the most critical environments in the hospital, in the ICU or ER. In school, I fell in love with the ICU and never really thought outside of a hospital setting. My sister called me one day and said, "I know what you want to do with your life!" And I said, "You don't know what I want to do with my life!" She said, "Yeah, you want to do disaster relief medical missions!" And in a 5-minute phone call, that dream was born and I've pursued it ever since.

A Doctor's Perspective (Dr. Mark Agness):

"Cease striving and know that I am God; I will be exalted among the nations. I will be exalted in the earth." - Psalm 46:10 (NASB)

My name is Mark Agness. I grew up in the Bay Area of California and attended Stanford University. I went east for medical school and residency and met my wife, Melisa, in Charlotte, NC. After service with the Air Force, we returned to California to raise our two sons and practice Emergency Medicine. My oldest is a graduate student at UC Berkeley in development economics and my youngest lives in rural Peru as an engineer pursuing sustainable agriculture. Melisa and I have served in Ethiopia with World Medical Missions. I have done short term medical mission trips to Mexico, Bulgaria, Kenya, and Ethiopia.

There frequently exists in me a sense of restlessness and uncertainty. My thoughts range widely and seem contradictory at times. I wonder if I missed or ignored God's call at some point in my life as I pursued my ambitions. I ponder whether my current path is of God's choosing or mine and whether I am able to change its direction. I find myself alternately grateful for God's remarkable provision and answer to my prayers and frustrated at the seemingly secular nature of my profession and my execution of its duties.

Upon my wife Melisa's retirement, this restlessness grew. I felt constrained to continue to work to provide health insurance for us both but also frustrated that my biological clock was "ticking" and that my health might not allow me to pursue God's calling, should it come, if I were to wait too long to answer it. I pondered Jesus' warning to the would-be disciple who balked at following until he had buried his father. "Follow me, and let the dead bury their own dead." Matthew

8:22 (NIV) Was this my warning (or had it been for years previous)?

We were preparing to go to Malawi (a country in southeast Africa). I blocked time from work intending to spend a month there. It was an opportunity for Melisa and I to serve together in a hospital that seemed to need both of our services. The preparation, as we approached departure, seemed a little unsettled. Our contact was out of the country and the addition of another short-term medical visitor made the chemistry of the visit even less certain. A conference call with all parties left both Melisa and I with a feeling that this wasn't meant to be. We both felt called to contact Soddo Christian Hospital in Ethiopia. We had both served there the year before and felt our services were appreciated. A recent email indicated a need and desire for a visit from us. We were met with open arms and the details of our trip were changed. Ethiopia rather than Malawi. Settled.

As we prepared to visit a different country and address a completely different set of needs, I received an email from Michelle Yates. Michelle is a remarkable clinician at Soddo Christian Hospital and has an amazing servant's heart. She is unfailingly humble and has proven skillful in redirecting my raw enthusiasm to serve into areas that would actually be useful and helpful at Soddo. She mentioned three new ventilators in their ICU and asked if I would assist in training. This is not an area of comfort for me. As an ER doctor, I manage airways and initiate ventilator settings, quickly turning over long-term management to the RTs and ICU doc. I swallowed and agreed, understanding that I would need to spend a little time relearning a skill from my training years, thirty years previous.

I researched the ventilators and spent nights on my i-pad using YouTube to shake the rust off my ventilator management skills and try to learn what had changed in the past thirty years. The answer was that lots had changed and that I was pretty rusty. In the evenings prior to our departure, Melisa would hear me listening to ventilator lectures and wondered what possessed me to immerse myself in oh-so-dry lectures on something I didn't really do. I didn't really have a good answer other than that I was being dutiful. God had other ideas.

As we approached departure for Ethiopia, the Coronavirus epidemic began to spread from Asia to Europe. Africa seemed little affected and our preparations continued with every intent of serving at Soddo. I read news stories about the impact of the virus in Northern Italy, in passing, but spent little time pondering it. We had other plans that didn't include Europe. Addis Ababa (the capital and largest city in Ethiopia) reported its first cases. Given the state of testing and medical care in Ethiopia, I realized this was probably just the tip of the iceberg. Flights from China continued unabated (to the tune of 30 daily into Addis). Chinese involvement in Ethiopia and other African nations is remarkable currently and the thought that travel would continue from China to Ethiopia during the pandemic seemed hard to fathom, but continue it did.

We were scheduled to leave on a Sunday. On the Thursday prior, the US embassy in Addis sent out travel warnings and I received an email from a contact at Soddo asking us if we were still planning to come. I had some angst about the possibility of becoming "stuck" in Ethiopia if the airports closed but indicated that we still planned our visit. We were informed that Soddo had cancelled all short-term visitors and that anybody with fever or respiratory symptoms would be quarantined for two weeks. We still planned to travel but concern was building. On Friday, the Ethiopian government began to enact restrictions to travel and more vigorous screening at Bolle Airport. The possibility of not being able to get to Soddo or return after four weeks became very real. In what was one of the biggest disappointments of my life, I agreed to cancel the trip just two days before departure.

I was angry, disappointed, and discouraged. All the preparation, prayer, time, change in destinations, and now (what I perceived) a "wasted" four-week hiatus from work seemed intolerable. I wasn't pleasant to be around. It was a long night with some "hard" prayers.

How God and Melisa tolerated me, I have no idea.

The very next day, on Saturday, Samaritan's Purse put out a call for a DART team to go to Northern Italy to operate a respiratory care unit. I knew immediately that I was meant to respond. I had previously been called for DARTs but my schedule got in the way and I had problems covering shifts. This time I had four weeks off. What little I knew about COVID-19 was discouraging. It seemed to have a predilection for "older" patients. I had just entered that demographic. Moreover, it favored males. Yet through this God gave me a sense of peace. In fact, I had never been so at peace with a decision. I responded and quickly received a call confirming plans to send me to Cremona, Italy for 4+ weeks. God was clearly directing my steps.

Yet God's providence didn't end here. Though I had no way of knowing it at the time, our hospital would have an ICU which would accept some of the sickest patients from the local hospital. We would have up to ten patients on ventilators in our unit. As it turned out, the lead doctor was a cardiologist who had ICU experience. The other providers (two retired ER docs, and one retired outpatient internist) had little recent ICU or ventilator experience. The lead doctor would, by necessity, work days. He needed a counterpart to manage the ICU at night.

I spent the next five weeks managing ventilated patients twelve hours a night in an ICU setting. My nights on YouTube had been rewarded with, at least, some didactic knowledge. Previous training, though distant, proved very helpful. Experience in the ER managing the sickest patients was priceless. Providence indeed. God had prepared me for this task.

A Doctor's Perspective (Dr. Bob Spencer):

Bob was raised in Mississippi and attended undergraduate studies at Mississippi College and medical school at the University of Mississippi. He met his wife, Linda, in Phoenix where they were both in post graduate studies. He practiced internal medicine and cardiology in Wisconsin and then at the University of Tennessee at Knoxville before moving to Pensacola, Florida where they now live with their twin sons.

He understands that God prepared him for his second career of missionary medicine through the diverse practice styles he has experienced. From the teaching responsibilities at the University of Tennessee to the extremes of rural healthcare in outreach clinics in Wisconsin and Alabama, God placed him in situations that prepared him for later service. He has since traveled to Kenya, Zimbabwe, Democratic Republic of Congo, Togo, the Bahamas and Italy, serving in resource rich and resource poor environments. His passion is to share his God-given knowledge with the healthcare providers around him. But more importantly, to spread the gospel of Jesus Christ to the least and the lost.

COVID-19 has been in the headlines now for several months. We saw how it affected China and then we saw that Italy was the most severely affected of Europe. Just as quickly, anxiety began to build in the US and numbers in the rest of the world became old news.

On Sunday morning March 16th I received a text about a DART deployment, and as a member, I responded to it indicating my availability. DART members never really know what we might be treating or where we may be going or when the call will come. But we are always ready with our bags packed. At 5PM I got a call and agree to respond. By 9AM on Monday I was at the airport.

My first leg was to North Carolina, where I would meet the rest of the first wave deployment team. When I arrived at the hotel, it was like old home week, as I met many of my colleagues from my prior training and/or deployment. We caught up with each other and then had a briefing in the lobby of the hotel. We learned we would be going to Italy and setting up a respiratory care unit (RCU); a specialized field hospital to treat lung disease.

We will be somewhere outside of Milan, the epicenter of COVID-19 in Europe, but details are still in the making. We will be the first ones in. Everyone else is fleeing to get out. The next morning 30 of us board Samaritan's Purse DC-8 with tons of cargo and take off on our 10-hour flight. We don't know where we will land. Some speculation was that we would have to land in Switzerland and truck into Italy. And we don't know if and when we will ever get a return ticket home. You see, all flights back to the USA are being cancelled.

As we land, I see empty streets out of the window. Even though it is 10:30PM, the streets are completely empty. Even the interstates are empty. It's a ghost town. We land at a normally busy, but now deserted airport and are bused to customs to get our passports stamped. We leave the lobby of the airport through the emergency exit, with the alarm blaring, to get back on the bus to return to the plane. When we get to the plane, the Italian Air Force has unloaded it, and we are off to our hotel for the night. The 1 ½ hour trip takes 2 ½ hours. I get settled into the hotel at 3AM and I am up at 5 to meet for our briefing.

The next morning, we pile on the buses and are taken to an empty parking lot next to a hospital. We are told they have converted this hospital into only COVID-19. They had less than 72 hours to get all the non-Covid patients out so the region could send all their Covid patients. They have 450 beds with over 500 patients. And so far, not a single ventilated patient has survived. As we unload the equipment and begin to set up the hospital, the gravity of the task sets in. We will be opening a 10 bed ICU for ventilator patients in addition to the 58 ward patients. We have two days to get it ready to accept patients.

The Italian people poured out their generosity. We were covered in their gratitude. The common message from them was "we thought we were alone, that no one cared. Even the other European nations did not come to help. Then you came, and we see that there is hope." The military, local hospital and civil authority worked with us to set up the hospital. We were ready to open in under 48 hours.

After three days of travel and hard work, I turn to someone beside me, and asked, "Do you know what city we are in?" You see, I am typically a control freak. I have to know where I am going. I will Google Earth it, study it, plan my route, and have full knowledge of every facet of the travel. But here, I just gave it all to God, I let go. I followed the Holy Spirit and where He led me. I gave it to Him. No fears, no anxiety, no worries when I was told I might not get home. And so, three days later, asked where am I and was content when the person beside me did not know either.

After inspections and a formal ceremony at midafternoon, we opened. I went to the Cremona hospital for our first patient and into what I thought was the ICU, only later to learn it was the recovery room. You see, they have an 8 bed ICU and now have 54 ICU patients. So the recovery room is part of the ICU. We find our ventilator has a different O2 connector than theirs. So, we have to use their ventilator to bring the patient over to our ICU. No problem, we adapt on the fly. They speak Italian and I speak English. With hand gestures, we get by. It's quick. They are stressed and overworked. We take what they give us and go with it. I return for the second patient, and the bed of the first patient is already filled with a new patient. I then realize I was in the recovery room for the first patient and I am asked to go to OR 8 for the next patient. In OR 8, there are three patients on ventilators. The enormity before us and what these people have been enduring for a month is beyond words. I remember to pray and invite the Holy Spirit into the room to guide the nurse and doctors and to give them comfort and rest.

3 IN THE BELLY OF THE WHALE

March 21, 2020

What do you do when you realize you are Jonah in the belly of the whale? How do you feel when you KNOW you've put yourself in harm's way? This virus looks menacing enough, but it is silent until it latches hold of its victims.

Well, you pray. You pray and you pray and you pray. I am at God's mercy and He decides whether I live or die. I thank Him that Samaritan's Purse is providing us with as much protection as they can, but as Dr. Lance Plyler once said in DART training, when we go on deployment, we realize even more, how our lives are in God's hands.

Tonight, our crew will arrive in Italy on the front lines of this horrible virus. "Lord, bring healing. Bring and cover us with Your protection."

"We are one hour out of Verona Airport"

Fear. Fear is a funny thing. If you dwell on it, if you let it capture your heart or your breath, it will overtake you. I just heard that all flights have been suspended, including Samaritan's Purse DC8 (the plane I traveled to Italy on!). And my heart stops. Immediately fear tries to invade my peace and it is not shy about it. I think, "Do I tell my husband this news?" "What if I'm here for too long?" Worry is experiencing something before it happens. I cannot succumb to this fear. I HAVE to trust that God sees me and is intimately involved in the affairs of my life.

I hit the ground running. I actually don't remember when I arrived at the camp or the hotel. Only that we arrived – tired – but running on faith and adrenaline. Quickly, we were shown the proper procedures on donning and doffing. My coworker, Barb, who arrived earlier in the week, showed me everything I needed to know and, like everyone who just arrived, we just started to work.

Morning of March 23, 2020

Pretty good night's rest. I dream of Coronavirus. I then pray in my dreams. "Lord, be with the daughters who called about their fathers."

We are doubling our beds this week. We have 30 beds that are filled, with male and female wards and an ICU. Hardest thing is wearing the PPE. Masks, two gloves, gown, head-covering, goggles or face-shield. All is sprayed with 0.5% chlorine water. It's hard to breathe and hard to see. "God, go with me this day."

I see Italian flags flying from windows and Italian laundry hanging out to dry. Life, though, seems to have virtually stopped here. The streets are so quiet. SP graciously got us all warmer clothing (I believe much was donated by an Italian company!) It's been very cold in the mornings and in the night. An Italian man donated all our hotel rooms! SP and Italy have been very good to us.

Evening of March 23, 2020

Super tired. Not much time to do anything. We wear our PPEs and are extremely careful. Already I miss my family and am counting the days. A very generous Italian man donated our hotel… hot showers and his chef (Andrea Roccato Catering)! May God richly bless him.

Post deployment thoughts: "As we don our PPEs, we each check each other. Do we have any wisps of hair sticking out from our hairnet? Did you remember your gloves? Is your gown fully tied and covering your scrubs? And invariably someone shouts, "Kelly, can you offer a prayer for us?!" It is one more vital layer of protection.

Evening March 24, 2020

"Please Lord, let the days go by quickly. I miss my family so much. You have been so gracious to me. My Savior forever."

Today we had beautiful weather and the time passed by much quicker. I believe the nurses have the toughest jobs on this deployment but everyone, and I mean everyone, works so hard here. All the people I have worked with here are the cream of the crop! And there are so many on this team working hard. Getting the tents up and ready, logistics, providing water, providing oxygen and electric, heat, etc. It's a huge undertaking and this team is prepared and in full work-mode!

The Coronavirus seems to be slowing here. A few days ago, 793 deaths a day. Then a day later 650, now 601. Now things are getting tougher in the US. I am concerned, though not worried, but very prayerful for my immediate family spread over Florida, Texas and Colorado.

A Nurse's Perspective (Taylor Pitkin):

The field hospital was built in the parking lot of Cremona Hospital, a 600-bed facility that had transformed into a 500-bed COVID-19 hospital only maintaining their labor and pediatric wards for those specialties. We learned they typically had capacity for 8 ventilators on their ICU and had 37 the day we arrived—none of those patients to date had been successfully weaned off the ventilators. There were 75 patients on CPAP and all the remaining patients had oxygen requirements. ORs, holding rooms, PACUs, and other spaces were crowded with patient beds to accommodate the overwhelming demands. We learned that 10% of Cremona Hospital staff themselves had contracted the virus and many of their employees had not had a day off in weeks. The streets of the city were beautiful but missing the people. Ambulance sirens were a noise with which we became all too accustomed—they could be heard on and off every day and night. A constant reminder of the silent enemy.

A Doctor's Perspective (Dr. Mark Agness):

"He has showed you, O man, what is good. And what does the Lord require of you? To act justly and to love mercy and to walk humbly with your God." Micah 6:8 (NIV)

It was hard to know what to expect. It was clear what the outside world thought of the Lombardy region of Italy. It was the epicenter of the Coronavirus epidemic in Europe. It was the site of death and despair. It was a place to be avoided. As I made my way to Italy, this pervasive perception was reinforced. At SFO, trying to catch a flight to Munich, I was pulled aside when my final destination was noted. Milan? "Italy is closed," was the response of the ticket agent at the gate. "No ma'am, it's not closed. I'm serving with Samaritan's Purse on a humanitarian mission." After delay, consultation, and further questioning I was allowed to pass with a shrug and the impression that I was beyond nuts. Indeed.

Upon arrival in Munich, a similar reception by the border control agent. In excellent English, "What is your destination?" When I explained that it was Milan, I was met with similar skepticism. Italy, and Milan in particular, was not a destination. It was a place to avoid. It was a place to read about in the news but certainly not a place to visit. It was the place where this virus lived and people died. The agent required not only an explanation but took my phone with the correspondence from Samaritan's Purse that explained the purpose of my travel. Another "Bless your heart…" moment (the blessing southerners confer on the confused and stupid) and I was allowed to pass.

Munich was where I began my ongoing struggle with the N-95 mask. Alitalia Airlines required the mask for travel to Milan and other destinations in Italy. Though I'd worn it before in training and rarely in patient care, I'd never worn the mask for extended periods. It was miserable. It made my nose run, pinched my nose shut, gave me a sense of claustrophobia and shortness of breath, and ultimately caused my throat profile of the disease it was meant to prevent. It hurt. It was tight. It gave me a headache. Yet all this seemed preferable to the disease, particularly as we got closer to the incubator in northern Italy.

Milan and the trip to Cremona were a blur. The ancient city of

Cremona was most notable for its silence and stillness. With the exception of the occasional work vehicle, dog walker, and ambulance the city was largely empty. To further the sense of the surreal, the sound of ambulance sirens was, seemingly, constant. Yet, in all of this, our reception was warm, gracious, and generous. Our plan to stay in tents on the site of the RCU (respiratory care unit) was met with the donation of hotel accommodations, a chef, and wonderful Italian food. In fact, the Italians, in their most challenging time, found ways to accommodate and shower us with their generosity. We were humbled by their sense of common good and brotherhood.

The arrival of the Samaritan Purse DC-8, at a time when the Italian people, and particularly those in Northern Italy, felt isolated and abandoned, was a glimmer of hope. Comments from citizens, filtered through the Italian media, bore this out. The fact that an organization would commit to willingly come to assist them in their time of trouble with altruistic motives was not lost on the community. The sense of hope and community in this act was palpable and felt by those of us volunteering, as well as those of this Italian community. The military was sent to help us erect our tent city. Local business owners volunteered services to help with our comfort and logistics. Citizens contributed anything they could to help us deal with the challenges of living and working in tents.

As the weather became cold, we were told that a local business had donated jackets for our use in the RCU. Dozens of jackets. As we shivered to remove our PPE at night, our "build" team devised a hot water system to supply the doffing tents. A local man brought his fork lift and spent each night resupplying tents, moving equipment, and filling diesel tanks for the generators. The local culinary society provided each volunteer with a box of local products (candy, baked goods, fruits, cheese) for Easter. Chocolate proliferated and we all feasted on locally produced chocolate Easter eggs. Our patients received foam mattresses to pad their cots. The build-team built awnings to allow for shade during the day for those patients who were able to sit outside. In all, the outpouring of generosity and brotherhood was amazing and reflected the mission of SP, as told by Jesus in the parable of the Good Samaritan in Luke 10. No political agendas, no desire for payment or recompense, no need for recognition, no gain. The gift is the reward to the giver and the recipient's response more than adequately compensates.

As we responded in mercy and humility, the vitality of God's spirit was revealed in both giver and recipient. This was God's grace, enacted through His servants, at its finest. Italy was not closed. It had never been more open.

4 TRUST JESUS, TRUST THE SCIENCE

Night March 25, 2020

I am tired but I can't think about it. I miss home… but I can't think about that either. I have to just forge ahead. I ask God for supernatural ability because I don't have it on my own. I'm not that old, just 57… but I know I can't do this without His help. Today, I had a momentary FEAR of the COVID virus. I know bad things can happen to good and godly people sometimes. I've just been praying and reading scripture and asking God to bring me home safely and well. My life and the lives of all my loved ones are in His hands.

I take phone calls from Italian daughters and granddaughters asking about their fathers and grandfathers. It's heartbreaking. Some of the patients have lost the will to live. Their bodies are failing them. Their lungs become damaged, as well as their kidneys. Some want to fight and some are just tired. If they pass away, their families will not be able to say goodbye, they will not be able to see their bodies to say goodbye. I have never seen anything like what is happening now in our collective world. Though I know tragedies have occurred throughout my life, I have been far-removed from it all.

Post deployment thoughts: "When in the ICU, I would see the nurses quietly tending to their ofttimes comatose patients, as their ventilators breathed for them. They would speak quietly to them, stroke their hair. And on the off-chance that their patient woke, they would encourage them to cough or breathe in deeply! Those nurses have hearts straight from the heart of God."

Post deployment thoughts May 5, 2020: I read over my journal and this project. I'm listening to the hymn "He Will Hold Me Fast" by Matt Merker. Suddenly, I break down crying. Suddenly, I realize He has held me fast. He brought me home. And some (patients) went home to Him. We are all still processing and may be for a long time yet.

Morning March 26, 2020

I am settling in on my days, but Oh, I miss home, my husband and family. Lord, watch over them all.

March 26, 2020

In the quiet moments in the lab, I thought I'd write some thoughts… First, I cannot begin to express the generosity of people in times of trouble. I can't begin to express how well we are treated by SP. We have been treated like royalty. From the start of our deployment, and catching our DC8 plane (Franklin Graham's son and granddaughter came out to greet us and pray with us early in the morning.) The DC 8 crew treated us so well (we even had our own Flight Attendant on the cargo plane!). Everything has been thought of… from our PPEs and our safety…to hot coffee, tea, and hot chocolate. A generous Italian man donated our hotel rooms (the staff cannot thank the anonymous donor enough!) and even provided his Chef to us. We have hot breakfasts and dinners and a delicious lunch is delivered from the hospital. We have HOT showers! In this cold weather, we might otherwise be sleeping in tents with cold weather, and in previous deployments, that is what we have done. God has provided everything we need and more! When I first arrived, Med Tech Barb Rash greeted me with an extremely warm greeting. Barb and I trained together at the 1st DART training and we briefly saw each other in Ecuador. She and the first wave crew had our entire hospital set up within days. She is older than me, so I don't know how she managed on her own. She certainly did not have it easy in the first few days, sleeping in below freezing weather one night! The weather here has been mostly beautiful in the days (cold… in the 40s and 50s) and in the night VERY cold! (In the 30s). You can tell Spring is on its way. One day we had extreme gusts of wind, so it felt like the tents might fly away! We've had a few power issues, but mostly everything is working amazingly well! After this first week, operations are coming together very well! SP has very carefully chosen the best and brightest staff, as far as I can tell. Everyone from the WASH team, to IT, to Operations, nurses, doctors – they are excellent at their jobs! My biggest prayer is safety for the team. Joey Garner (Member Care/Manager/Chaplain with SP) said to me on the plane (and I so appreciated it!), "Trust the science." Meaning, as we use our PPE, our 0.5% chlorine wash, stepping out of our scrubs before we leave for hotel, wearing our masks constantly, and washing our hands often, trust. It's Trust Jesus, and Trust the science. Pastor Hans has been sharing devotionals every morning and he will be leaving tomorrow. I appreciated something he said this morning… that we trust Jesus with our very lives. We give Him permission to do whatever He might allow… bringing us home to health…or we go to meet Him. I have little absolute control in any of this, as does anyone in the world at this moment. In my lifetime, I have never seen a worldwide disaster like this, one that has incited fear into so many people. Our financial systems… life as most of us know it...everything has changed. Here in Italy, the death toll has gone slightly down. I am praying the curve is beginning a downward trend. Just days ago, on March 24th, Italy saw its highest death toll. Looking at the numbers, I felt that maybe the toll will be close to flatlined in 3 weeks…but now I feel it might take a little longer. I am scheduled to leave back for the US around April 18th. Currently we are scheduled to fly into Washington, DC and then home to quarantine for two weeks. I am praying that we can make it home. Before I left from the US, I lost my job on a Friday. On a Sunday morning, I got a text from SP to come here. Though it is hard, I knew in my heart, I was supposed to come. My third son also lost his job (his coworkers also lost their jobs). Our daughter's line of work is affected. When I get home, as I can currently tell, the US will be at its peak of coronavirus.

So, a little of what it's like being in the PPE. We wake up in freezing weather, catch the bus and arrive just minutes away to the hospital grounds. We walk a bit and change into our proper chlorinated scrubs and big rubber boots. We walk a bit more (I call it "walking the gauntlet") to the open tents which are open on each end to the lovely cold weather (make that bitter cold weather haha) and don our PPE gear. First gloves, then gown, then mask, then second pair of gloves, then hairnet – making sure all wisps of hair are covered, then face-shield or goggles. Then walk to our proper tent. If you wear goggles, you might have difficulty because the goggles constantly fog. If you wear a face-shield and the N95 mask, you might feel like you are suffocating (and you might be). We do get breaks from time to time, but essentially you wear your gear for twelve-hour shifts or longer. Now as a Lab Tech, I am exposed to blood and other bodily fluids, which are mostly contained (and I say mostly, because many times we are exposed, but can quickly remedy the situation, by rinsing with 0.5% chlorinated water). In our job, we need to practice caution and we use excellent protocol, but our risks are still high. However, as I go into the tents with the nurses and doctors, I am overwhelmed at the amazing people who are serving the sick. There are not enough masks for the patients, and they need to cough all day and night… The nurses and doctors are very much exposed. These guys are complete heroes to me. They are amazing. I brought some typed scriptures to encourage me in the "hot" zone, and they have calmed my fears and reminded me all over again of God's care for us. One of my favorite scriptures in this time is Psalms 55:18. "He hath delivered my soul in peace from the battle that was against me, for there were many with me." (KJV)

When you hang onto God's words, which are true and absolute, you will find comfort for your soul.

We have an ICU here which I believe has 10 beds. Everyone there is on a ventilator. Some of the patients have spunk, and if spunk alone could heal them, they might get out of here. A few have no fight left in them. The hardest thing is when I receive a call from a daughter, son or grandchild. They want to know how their loved one is. I remember when my Dad was sick and how heartbroken I was. Going through that experience when my Dad was dying, I believe, has given me an ability to empathize with these daughters and granddaughters. Short of miracles, which can happen, some may not be going home to their families. Currently in the hospitals here, which are overrun with patients, no one can visit their loved one. If they die, they cannot see the body and grieve. There have been so many deaths in this region that funerals have become difficult to do. One lady shared how she got sick and had to go to the hospital. When she recovered, she went home to find that her husband had died at home. I can't even imagine that kind of suffering.

Post-Deployment thoughts: As I walked into the ICU every day or night (depending on my shift), I zeroed in on those patients. Sometimes, I had received an earlier call from a loved one asking about their parent or grandparent. Each one I silently prayed for. Many times, just before a shift change, a patient passed. That was the hardest. Especially for the nurses and doctors. They lovingly prepared the body. They soberly prepared the necessary paperwork. Doctors acquired a translator to call the family and deliver the most difficult of news. Our doctors were amazing, and offered the most comforting words they could - "that their loved one did not die alone and that they were very cared for."

We have two female wards and two male wards. These patients look well, but are still very sick. Obviously, some are very bored being stuck in these wards. Some would just like to leave, but the police would have to be notified, according to the Italian law at this time. Such are our times during this coronavirus. Everyone is ordered to be quarantined. We have no children in these wards. I am so thankful this disease has spared them. My friends who served in Iraq experienced the worst images of war... the maiming and death of beautiful children. My coworker and friend, Barb, spoke of her time in Iraq... and how one little girl needed blood. Barb had shouted out to her coworker for him to get blood from her toes...and in shock, he replied "she had no toes." The team loved on this little child and found her pacifier which was still under her clothes. Barb lovingly washed it and gave it back to her to comfort her. God bless the hands that minister to the broken.

A Nurse's Perspective (Taylor Pitkin):

By the Lord's grace, we were able to open and start taking patients within two days. Our capacity included 60 ward beds and 10 ICU beds to help offload the burden from Cremona Hospital. One of the unique challenges that we faced at first was patients who were scared to be sent to the "tent hospital." Patients and their family members were skeptical of the care and treatment they would receive, as well as the conditions in which they would be living. When you are not accustomed to sleeping on a cot or having a shared space with multiple other patients, I can imagine it would seem overwhelming and unfair when you're set up in the parking lot of a large, modern hospital, even in the midst of a virus that is overwhelming the healthcare system. The ways that God responded to this were extraordinary…The tents were supplied with heating and cooling units, oxygen capacity for every bed, and there was a manufacturing plant that within the span of a few days made custom mattresses for every single cot. Patients came over aporetic, but very quickly felt and received the love that was being poured out on them in the tents— and most of all prayer for these patients to heal. We witnessed the Holy Spirit at work in these tents.

A Nurse's Perspective (Shannon Wood):

If I could describe my feeling during this time, it would be love. I have never experienced so much love for patients than I have here. I feel like my love for people and patients grows every day. It's a special situation in there; that these patients are in the ICU for a long time because of how sick they are. You really get to know them. You really get to understand who they are and I LOVE my patients like nobody's business. That love is fueled by God because there is enough tragedy, there is enough struggle, there are enough difficult situations that, I personally, my own love would be exhausted. To have God fill me up every single morning and to combine my passion with His love for these people and to be a channel of that… and to let Him use me to love patients, there is nothing like it.

A Doctor's Perspective (Dr. Mark Agness):

"Cast all your anxiety on Him because He cares for you." 1 Peter 5:7 (NIV)

"Do not be anxious about anything, but in everything by prayer and supplication with thanksgiving let your requests be made known to God." Philippians 4:6-7(ESV)

The surroundings are vaguely familiar. Patients in beds with endotracheal and nasogastric tubes. Monitors displaying cardiac rhythm, pulse oximetry, pulse, and blood pressure. Intravenous pumps with various drips, vasopressors, sedatives, and antibiotics. The sounds, too, are familiar. The nearly incessant sound of alarms from the various machines, ventilators, and monitors. Yet the setting is very different. We are in a large tent. The patient beds are lightweight, portable cots designed for use in remote settings, the lighting is from fluorescent rope lights strung overhead, and the negative pressure ventilation system is an ingenious construct of flexible ducting slung from the central support creating a bright yellow caterpillar above. The exhaust below pulls the air out through a large HEPA filter creating an environment where viral particles and respiratory droplets are actively removed from the tent.

It's noisy. The exhaust system, with added propane-driven heaters at night, creates a continuous background of mechanical noise. The generators that drive all our systems are a constant rumble, and the alarms and beeping punctuate the night with the threat of a "crash" where a patient deteriorates. I'm working the night shift with five seasoned ICU nurses who remain continuously active tending to as many as ten patients in our unit.

Only the patients are silent. Each patient with an endotracheal tube and ventilator, surrounded by a cocoon of supportive wires, IV tubing, and monitors. Each patient, either in a chemically-induced rest or in a post-sedation stupor. We receive our patients from the adjacent hospital, where they are on multiple medications to allow tolerance of the mechanical ventilator. Our first activity is to try to allow them to awaken. We are finding that this process is neither quick nor reliable. Many patients remain obtunded, minimally responsive and profoundly weak for days if not weeks.

The first few nights in this environment were challenging. Creating a functional hospital for as many as 68 patients in a parking lot is no mean feat. Not only are the shelters makeshift but the need for heat, electricity, water, and in the case of a respiratory care unit, oxygen is critical. Our "build" staff has had lots of experience in creating similar makeshift hospitals but each situation is unique. The hospital in Cremona is no exception.

The nights are cold and the weather is not cooperating. The temperature drops below freezing and our heaters struggle to keep up. The patients in the wards request more blankets. The cots are uncomfortable and the environment is far from luxurious. As the night chills, the wind begins to blow. Hard. Our tents are designed to withstand significant wind but each tent has its challenges. If the supporting structure is not properly inflated (there are no tent poles, only pressurized supporting tubes), the cold air causes the pressure in the supports to drop and the tent becomes weakened. A call on the radio that one of the women's tents is collapsing, causes panic amongst patients and a flurry of activity from the build team. The nursing staff remains calm and the problem is remedied by re-inflating the supporting structure of the tent. Crisis averted.

We take power for granted until it's not there. Our first night in the ICU the lights went out. It's an eerie feeling. The only lights are from the ventilators that have a battery backup...thank God. A terse call on the radio and the breakers were reset.

The power went off again. The nurses scrambled to find "ambu bags" for each ventilated patient to assure the ability to provide "lungs" allowing the patients to breathe in the event of the batteries in the ventilators failing. The power returns only to fail again. Our engineers determine the issue is merely a matter of re-distributing the load and the power will stay on. Crisis averted.

In the hospital setting, we take oxygen supply for granted as well. At rest, we breathe 21% oxygen to maintain cellular function. No problem when our lungs are healthy. The equation changes dramatically with underlying conditions like emphysema, pulmonary fibrosis, or in our case – COVID pneumonia. Our patients are not healthy and most require some oxygen. Some demand a lot. Oxygen concentration now increases from 21% to 60, 80, or 100% with additional pressure support provided by the ventilator. In the first days, we operated on pressurized oxygen and large oxygen concentrators. Concentrators can provide ample oxygen for several ventilators with limited flow rates. Adjustments to the ventilators to compensate for limited flows were a challenge but manageable. The failure of a concentrator was a near catastrophe. During our power crisis, we damaged the electronics in one concentrator causing it to fail. Another alarm and scramble to make sure each patient supplied by the concentrator had ample oxygen. Juggling the "source" of the supply was a short-term solution but a longer-term solution would have to wait until the break of day.

The Italian people came through again and again, finding ways to serve not only us but their fellow citizens. The sense of shared purpose and brotherhood was both real and affirming. A medical equipment supplier donated the use of an oxygen supply and manpower necessary to create a one-inch copper line to provide for all of our wards and the ICU. This would be adequate to provide for a medium-sized hospital, let alone our RCU. Crisis averted.

Ventilators are designed to be reliable and adaptable. Neither characteristic is guaranteed and the paucity of ventilators was one of the driving issues behind our DART response. We arrived with ten small, portable units. The first ventilator failed on night two. Alarms alerted us to a drop in the patient's oxygen concentration. We switched to manually "bagging" the patient and attempted to return to the ventilator. Similar results. As it turned out the ventilator had suffered the same fate as the concentrator and was out for the duration. Fortunately, we had only eight ventilated patients at the time. Ongoing challenges with ventilator circuits, filters, and temperamental electronics cost us several more ventilators over the weeks to come. Resupply by SP and decreased demand at the hospital prevented us from making some very challenging ethical decisions; namely, which patient could be removed from the ventilator. Crisis averted.

What do we do when all the ventilators alarm at the same time? The staff had been briefed on our oxygen supply and backup. In a catastrophic failure we believed there was approximately 20 minutes of oxygen. Given our needs, this wasn't reassuring but we felt a catastrophic failure was unlikely. Early one morning, all the ventilators on one side of the tent alarmed with "Low Oxygen Pressure" alarms. Loss of oxygen pressure was tantamount to mass casualty and twenty minutes isn't much time to fix this problem. Going suddenly from 80 or 100% oxygen to room air, even with the assistance of a mechanical ventilator would end in death. A request for an urgent visit from our biomedical expert relieved our fears. We had "stressed" the system but there would be no failure. Crisis averted.

It seemed each night was a challenge of faith in which we were all reminded of Peter's call to "Cast all our anxieties on Him..." Paul is even more specific with the solution; "...by prayer and supplication, with thanksgiving, let your requests be made known to God…" And that is exactly what we did. In each instance, we were rewarded with a solution that met our stated need. Every time. Our anxiety was worldly and pragmatic. God's answer was invariably adequate and, in retrospect, predictable. Our earthly paradigm was inconsequential given the nature of the God we were serving. Paul reassures us in Philippians that the result of our acting in faith is the promise that "...the peace of God, which transcends all understanding, will guard your hearts and your minds in Christ Jesus." Philippians 4:7 (NIV)

Prayers were answered. Crises of faith were averted and God's peace did, indeed, descend on the RCU in Cremona, Italy. Amazing.

5 DONNING, DOFFING, REPEAT, REPEAT

March 27, 2020

I communicate with different lab workers at the Cremona hospital. I sent a mass message to six of them. One of them wrote me back: "Purtroppo sono a casa im quarantena perche positive a COVID." Translated: "Unfortunately, I am at home in quarantine because I am positive for COVID."

I feel so badly for them. I believe medical personnel all over are running out of masks. We are very, very protected…but this virus is microscopic (as are all). We have to be diligent and cautious as we put on our gear (donning) and as we take it off (doffing). The person in the lab who got COVID is young. I believe he will be okay. I saw his photo on WhatsApp. He has a little baby. This virus has put fear into so many. I will keep reading my scriptures, praying, taking my vitamin supplements and making every precaution to get home well to my family.

Psalms 103:1-5 (NIV) says, "Praise the Lord, my soul; all my inmost being, praise his holy name. Praise the Lord, my soul, and forget not all his benefits – who forgives all your sins and heals all your diseases, who redeems your life from the pit and crowns you with love and compassion, who satisfied your desires with good things so that your youth is renewed like the eagle's."

While I've been here… in the lab, the phone rings quite often. I answered, "Laboratory, this is Natalie. No Italiano." And invariably the person on the other end would say, "No English". Somehow, we managed to talk a little. One daughter (faglia) called about her father (padre). He was my dad's age, so I immediately felt endeared to the daughter AND to the father. The father didn't have much fight left in him. He wanted to go. But the nurses and doctors are committed to helping in whatever way to help them live and to make them comfortable. One of the nurses (Shannon Wood) rushed into the lab and was trying to get labs run on her patient. Later she came in just to cry because he passed away shortly after. She had taken such good care of him. These nurses and doctors are the finest. How they do this, I don't know. With God's comfort, they will be alright… but they sob quietly and then go back to work.

Post deployment thoughts: Can you imagine being the patient and all you can see are the eyes of your caregiver? What I find amazing is the love that the patients felt, in spite of our PPE. The nurses smile under those goggle and masks. They help clean the patients, and change their bedsheets. They encourage them to fight…to cough. Those nurses pray under their breath, BREATHE! The staff doesn't stop. They clean their bedpans, cover their patient with a clean blanket and in the early morning, new labs are drawn, as they gently wake them – hoping for better lab values than the day before.

So, more about COVID. Eighty percent of people who get it have MILD symptoms. It starts with fever, followed by a dry cough. After a week, you may have shortness of breath. It rarely causes a runny nose, sneezing or sore throat, though that's been observed in 5% of patients. Thirteen percent are severe, developing pneumonia and shortness of breath. Nearly 5% are critical with respiratory failure causing septic shock and organ failure.

Currently:

The US has 85K cases

Italy has 80K

China had 81K

Spain is next at 57K and Germany at 47K.

The US has 259 cases per million population, while Italy has 1333 cases per million population. This is why Samaritan's Purse deployed to Italy, because the need was so very great. At the time that I deployed here, the death rate was at its peak. That rate went down for 3 days in a row… and has gone up and down in the past week. The TREND on the curve IS going down, but slowly. I think 2-3 months, Italy may be over it. However, I believe that within one month, the US curve may continue to go up, just based on statistics, unless God in His mercy stops the virus. Of course, we are praying for our country and the world. Hardships are just that. Hard. They are awful. Tragedies are awful. But in the midst of these great hardships are beautiful acts of humanity. The priest in Italy, whose parishioners bought him a ventilator… but he gave it up to help save a young patient. And recently we heard about a doctor here in the hospital who was an atheist. He watched as one of his patients, a pastor, read the Bible to the sick. He and his coworkers heard the Bible being read. The pastor did die, but the doctor and his team have said they have gone back to the faith of their parents. They have been comforted by the words of God.

Well, nothing like feeling old here. However, I am probably a median age of much of the staff. We have the very young (in the 20s age group) and we have the older 50+, it seems. EVERYONE here is so brave! EVERYONE here has had the best attitude!

I have had a few moments of panic. Am I coughing? Oops, I have some chest pain. My back hurts… Thankfully we are taking our temperatures every morning and every evening. I am being ultra-diligent about eating healthy and taking my supplements. Today, I gave good laugh to some of the young nurses. I stepped into a tent and my awkward boot caught something and I tripped. I tried to gracefully land, but I landed on my right knee. Ouch.

We sound a bit spoiled here and we are, I suppose. I count it a huge blessing for all of us, as this deployment has some tough segments to it. It is end of week one (and week two) for some, and believe me, these guys are more than rock-stars! They work 12-13 hour shifts.

Mike Liner, the Pharmacist, who I worked with in Ecuador, eats and sleeps here, 24/7, as he is the only Pharmacist. Everyone here has family back in the States and we all consider that when we head back to the hotel… they are very much on our hearts and minds. Kelly Sites, one of our directors, has a daughter in the states who works in the health field. She has some cold symptoms, much like COVID. Everyone here has concerns at home, and they are brave.

Today, we had a lovely lunch with lots of carbs. I "accidentally" ate some. Then I wanted to fall asleep on the job. We are all tired and the one thing we keep saying is, God has us. He is the strength of my heart and my portion forever. And He gives power to the faint.

A Nurse's Perspective (Shannon Wood):

I'll tell you a story. The first week I was here, I took care of this one patient. He was my first patient that I took care of and I worked sooo hard to help him get better, and he didn't stand much of a chance to be completely honest. He was elderly. He had other issues… comorbidities we call them; other issues that were wrong with his body before he got the virus. And he stood very little chance. Well, he slowly started to get better and he started to wake up. I loved on him like nobody's business. He and I developed a small relationship of just being his family. He even spoke a little bit of English, so I was able to communicate with him a little more than I was with other patients and that was a blessing. One day he took a turn for the worse and got very, very sick. He died within a day of getting sick. It was incredibly hard for me as a person to deal with losing him and having his family not be there. Losing him and loving him even as a friend or family member myself, so I grieved that. I talked with another nurse here who helped me process the grief of losing my first patient here at this ICU. She first of all let me know it was okay to grieve this; this was a sad situation. She helped me understand it was okay to love my patients this deeply. She prayed for me that day, that I would not love my patients any less for the fear of losing them and for the fear of experiencing the same grief again. Through her prayers and my commitment to make that real, I intentionally loved my patients harder, knowing that the grief and struggle was worth it and that Jesus, not me, would sustain me through the hardship of losing patients again - which we did lose patients again. This disease is a horrible disease. But I have never regretted a single time that I've held a patient's hands, and stroked their head, and in my broken Italian saying, "Tutto andra bene" (everything will be okay). Jesus used my nursing friend to help me continue strong and praying for me in that way and also pointing me to the One who would help me sustain the grief and suffering that I was going to continue to face in the many weeks that I was here. I feel like that was a turning point for me, that I was able to see death and grief early on and know how to handle it through the strength of Christ and Christ alone. There have been plenty of tears cried here. I love Italy.

A Doctor's Perspective (Dr. Mark Agness):

"Put on the full armor of God, so that you can take your stand against the devil's schemes." - Ephesians 6:11 (NIV)

It's a bit of a stretch. PPE isn't exactly God's armor and I doubt it really helps against the devil's schemes, but it was a big part of the deployment in Italy and New York. Personal Protective Equipment (PPE) is a bucket phrase for all the things we wear to prevent transmission of infection. It's a common discussion item in hospital infection control committees. Taken to its extreme in laboratories and clinical situations like Ebola, it includes Tyvek suits and battery driven filter hoods. In Italy, it consisted of an N-95 mask, face shield or goggles, hair covering, a protective gown, two sets of gloves, and rubber boots worn over scrubs. All this equipment was either discarded, sterilized, or left behind at the end of the day. The goal of preventing exposure to active viral particles, either on surfaces or suspended in microdroplets was implied in the efforts taken to properly apply (don) and remove (doff) the equipment.

First, my "armor" was unpleasant. The N-95 mask, when worn for more than an hour caused headache, and pain across the bridge of the nose. No matter how I adjusted the straps, malleable nasal bridge, or used different masks, it remained uncomfortable. When worn for 12 hours, it seemed oppressive. Most of us ended up wearing band aids across the bridge of the nose to prevent erosions of the skin. Moreover, my facial armor caused my nose to run, gave me a post nasal drip and sore throat, and by its very nature, felt claustrophobic. I was short of breath and in need of "fresh air" immediately upon donning the mask. Unfortunately, most of these mask-related symptoms were common to the Coronavirus infection we were trying to avoid. The thought crossed all of our minds on numerous occasions. "Do I have it?" "Is this COVID?" The answer was a glorious "no" when the mask was removed and the symptoms resolved.

The act of donning our PPE was a ritual. Fitting the face shield or goggles, getting the gowns to cover most of the scrubs, making sure the pants were securely tucked into the boots, putting on two pairs of gloves in just the right way to "sandwich" the arms of the gown to prevent a skin gap at the wrists. One size fitting all was a euphemism for the gown "not really fitting anyone." And, writing our names on the mask or gown was helpful to address the challenge of identifying people by height or gait since the only visible feature in full PPE was the eyes. The inability to "read" facial expressions challenged communication and dehumanized us to some extent. Our patients only knew us by the sound of our voices and the name written on our PPE.

We usually came out of the "hot zone" once during the shift and at the end to the doffing tent to remove our PPE. This ritualized activity was even more important and time consuming. On night shift, it often occurred in the cold with temperatures dropping to or a little below freezing and our only clothing being scrubs. We became very efficient in the doffing process. No shortcuts, but very efficient. Moving from the doffing tent to a heated break tent in the green zone was a focused rush.

And bleach. The process of doffing required multiple washings and spraying with 0.5% bleach. *Wash the hands, remove the first gloves, wash the hands, remove the face shield, wash the hands, remove the hair covering, wash the hands, remove the gown, wash the hands….* until finally, we can step over the red line, remove the final pair of gloves and wash with soap and water. The calf burn - a linear horizontal skin burn just above the boot was evidence of overzealous spraying with bleach solution. Many of us sported this painful reminder throughout most of the deployment.

Yet with all of this ritual and attempt to avoid contamination, we would have been naive to believe that we could truly avoid the virus. Do the masks really fit and prevent virus from entering the airways? Many on our team "failed" the mask fit test. Because of the shape of their faces, they could breathe around the mask. Are we preventing aerosolized virus adequately? In the course of clinical care, we had to use unfiltered bag-valve masks, nebulizers, and allow patients with tracheostomies to cough. Viral-laden droplets were everywhere. This was probably even more the case on the wards where patients coughed freely and were not intubated. Virus was likely omnipresent. It was on our scrubs, our masks, our boots, and the skin exposed from the nape of the neck to the top of the gown.

And we breached. All of us. We tore gloves, got needle sticks, got up close and personal with patients shedding virus by the millions.

And yet, through all of this, we remained healthy. Our hospital was directly across the street from the larger hospital where 500 patients, all with COVID were hospitalized. Some of those patients were physicians and nurses who had contracted the illness during the course of their clinical responsibilities. How did we remain healthy over five weeks (and counting) working twelve hour shifts seven days a week? It's tempting to rationalize and suggest we had "better" PPE, better technique, or stronger bleach (it was strong…). But another answer seems more plausible given the implausibility of chance and good technique being the cause of our health. The major "armor" we were afforded consisted of prayer. Lots of it. We prayed, we were prayed over, prayed over others, asked for prayer, and recruited prayer partners from all over the world, literally.

We were prayed for throughout the US, Australia, Europe, Canada, and likely parts unknown to me. Although not clinically "provable", we all knew the risk and limitations of our PPE, and our personal failures to strictly follow protocols. We all knew there was protection beyond that offered by cloth coverings and bleach. None of us needed a study to prove it. The armor was effective and nigh impenetrable given the source.

6 I LOVE MY BOOTS!

March 28, 2020

Woohoo! It's Friday and Sunday's on its way! That means I'll start a new week and get closer to my second Friday. I am doing well. Fell twice this week. I popped my head into the break tent and promptly tripped in these mongo boots! It was comical but nurse Savannah Koop, was so sweet. She was laughing hard but trying not to, until she realized I was a grandma and she felt bad. Haha So she got me some Tylenol, God bless her! And Chaplains Jason and Damaris Scalzi made me some Cappuccino! So, it's "I've fallen and I can't get up without Cappuccino and Tylenol!" On a sad note, we can't take Excedrin. At all. No Ibuprofen, so keep that in mind you guys. It makes COVID worse if you are on it. We take our temperatures morning and evening. If Mom has a thermometer, she should take her temperature daily, morning or night. If not, someone please buy one and get it to her and Rick's Mom. It's important they take their temperature. And don't share thermometers at all. Honestly, it wouldn't hurt for everyone there to take their temperatures morning and night. Buy extra if you need to.

One of our EMTs (Becky) didn't look too well today and I'm concerned for her. She is a young mom and I pray for her. I think the hours are tough and she might need more rest. God is keeping me going. I kind of crashed yesterday. I think maybe we run on adrenaline and then are apt to crash. Maybe too much Italiano pasta and sweets for lunch. Mom would LOVE the pastries here. The amazing locals bring them to us fresh-baked several times a week! I thought I would lose weight here, but nope. Seriously, I eat well (meaning healthy) and rarely eat the pasta and bread, but it is AMAZING. No soft drinks here, thank God, or I'd be tempted. Just coffee and water. But on a bad note, I have become a Cappuccino drinker. Every morning at

10:30AM is 5:30AM your time.

So here is my schedule: Up at 5:45AM (not too bad), get dressed, go down three flights of stairs for a nice breakfast. Breakfast is eggs or oatmeal, bread and cheese (and Ashley, it is FRENCH-worthy cheese!), a polenta of sorts (like cheese corn muffins) and oranges and bananas. Then you can have coffee or hot tea. I do the hot tea (I might be British, Paul) and oats and definitely an orange every day. This is when I take my vitamins. Did you need to know this? Yes, you did. After/during breakfast, announcement and a devotional. Then by 6:45AM., we take the bus to the hospital grounds. It's a 3-minute bus ride. Just for safety, we don't touch anything on the bus. Then we arrive at our dressing tents and "don" our gear. This takes a little time. And then to work by 7AM. I work busy until around 10:30AM. I get out of these PPEs (personal protective equipment) and feel like I can breathe a little better! That takes a few minutes, because as I've mentioned earlier, we have to use 0.5% chlorine rinse in-between each item taken off. Our boots are even rinsed top and bottom. Then we can go into the green zone, but we still wear masks. I think probably the hardest thing about the masks (nothing else bothers me too much), is you have the sense that you can't fully breathe and then add a face-shield to that. Fortunately, the weather here has become more and more beautiful (Spring is coming) and I step out of the tent to breathe fresh air every so often. Then I take that break around 10:30AM… step into the break tent and fix a small Cappuccino that is keeping me going (and yes, honey, it's delicious and Starbucks-worthy). Sometimes, I'll have a power bar or FRESH HOMEMADE PASTRY that the locals keep bringing us! When in Milan, do as the Milaniers do!

Then back to the tent to re-don after break. Then around 1:30PM or 2, lunch has arrived. Usually a hot lunch and we "doff" our PPEs off again and go to lunch "clean". Lunch is always hot and healthy in day shift and sandwiches during the night shift. Take a restroom break then, because you might not get to later. Of course, we are all somewhat dehydrated, because we go easy on fluids so we won't have to break often. Then back into the tents to don your PPEs again. Last break might come around 4:30PM and push repeat, repeat. Then you hang in there til 7PM until TIME TO GO TO THE HOTEL! The bus doesn't leave for the hotel until 7:45PM. Hallelujah! We "doff" again… all the chlorine again. And we smell pretty bad by that time. Now, keeping in mind, most deployments don't get a hotel. Staff goes back to a tent full of the ladies or men they are working with and sleep on cots. They take a lukewarm, military style shower, but we have been blessed with wonderful beds and clean sheets! And HOT showers! And chef-prepared foods! It is truly a blessing! Then shower at the hotel (quickly), quick dinner, quick announcements… then time to WhatsApp each of you, then off to bed by 9:15PM, where I say goodnight to my darling husband!

Morning comes much too quickly and we start the whole process again. I try not to think of the days… and I don't think of the date. I am pushing for April 1st which will be here very shortly, and then I'll, God-willing, be headed home sometime around April 18th. It won't be long and I'll be at the halfway point. I know that all my family has suffered along with me. I'm sorry if I've worried the ones I love. I know God placed me here and the timing was right. I do sooo look forward to being home. I know this virus has really been something and it is JUST beginning in the United States. I just got word that Samaritan's Purse will be deploying soon in the US. They expect things to get worse of course. As of now… real-time, the US has 104,256 cases and 1704 deaths (at the time of printing June 2020, the US has 1.92 million confirmed cases and 110,000 deaths). The US is now currently the highest for cases…surpassing Italy, but I pray you will be encouraged. Only 5% of ALL cases in the world are serious or critical at this point. That's 1 out of 20 people…usually the elderly. So, if you have a mask, wear them around our moms. So important, because you could carry it and not know you have it.

From a medical standpoint, laboratory values show that WBC counts go up (Neutrophil count is up; Lymphs are down). C-Reactive Protein values are high in the 155-400 range, while LDH values are extremely high (290-821). BUN and Blood Urea values are out of range. Quite a few patients have glucose values that are very high. On the blood gases, Calcium seems to run low. AST values are running high.

March 29, 2020

Today was time change. One less hour of blessed sleep. So far, I am doing great. Busy morning getting labs out and they're not all ready… so waiting a bit. Getting the labs back from the Cremona Hospital and those guys are surely busy. Did I mention that one of the lab techs I talk to has COVID? He has a young baby. That is the part that makes me saddest. I thank God with all my heart that this virus is not currently focused on our children and grandchildren. I mentioned that a sweet old man (my dad's age) passed away. Broke my heart. How these nurses keep caring, I don't know, but they care and care for their patients…and when their patients die, they come in and have a good, private cry… and go back to work. The family cannot come and visit them. Can you imagine? When they pass, they do not get to see the body they loved. The daughter called me and I was able to tell her that her dad had the BEST nurse…who loved and cared for him…and that my Dad was her dad's age and I knew a little of how she felt. So heartbreaking.

The men have such beautiful names here in Italy. Valentino! Gianluigi! Giancarlo! Francesco! Giuseppe! Umberto! I just love saying them. And in Northern Italy, you say it with flair! The language is musical! It might be my favorite language, even better than French. No, it IS my favorite because it is a passionate language. So beautiful. In regards to my job as a Laboratory Technologist, I am not skilled at drawing blood and have never had a position doing it (mainly working in Toxicology), so the nurses have been drawing. They have trouble too sometimes, so watching them when they are having trouble getting a blood tube from a patient is difficult to watch! One older man was frail and the draw was painful. The nurse kept trying to get blood. The patient was quiet but gestured with his hand that he was in pain.

Sometimes in the medical field you encounter someone who has a great sense of humor! Kelly Arroyo is a nurse from California. She is a prayer-warrior and has a fun personality! It was morning and we are dragging our derrieres out of bed, eating breakfast... and catching the bus to work. We then walk a bit to our changing tent, where we put our BIG rubber boots on. Kelly bends over to put on her boots and says a repeated chant, "I love my boots... I love my boots." Cracked me up. We look like a motley crew. Maybe I should say those of us over 50 do. Actually, I should simply say, I do! haha I have this fly-away hair and have to pin it every which way to tuck it under my "hair-net". It's a lovely look. The young nurses look so cute, have long straight hair and when they take off their hair-net, every hair still in place! I think I look a wreck! My scrubs have been sent to the hospital to be laundered in hot chlorinated water and come back a total mess. But that is the least of my or anyone else's worries. We older ladies think of our families at home...our husbands...mothers... kids, grandkids and extended family. Gosh, older ladies. How did that happen? I miss you all!

Today the number of US cases are at 123K. New cases per 1 million people are 374. Seven deaths for every 1 million people, but total deaths are 2,229 attributed to COVID as of March 29. To give perspective, just 10 days ago on March 19, total deaths attributed to COVID were 206. Our 1st case in US was January 20th. In just 9 weeks, these numbers are staggering.

Total cases in Italy have reached 92K. Daily new cases are around 6000 a day. Total deaths have been 10000. You can imagine, their first case was only February 15th, a mere 6 weeks ago. Italy is somewhat the size of California...so this has spread exponentially here. The elderly have been the ones to get sick quickest. Most of the younger have recovered. It seems a factor that those who get sick may have a low immune response or have high blood sugar. The supplements that I am taking during this time is a multi-vitamin, Vitamin D, and I think I threw in some additional supplements including B12 and Zinc. I try to eat an orange a day and stay away from sugary sweets and breads, but that is hard here in Italy! I feel amazingly well. I am getting good rest, but there is nothing really in-between work and rest. We shower, eat, sleep, work, shower, eat, sleep, work. There's a wonderful camaraderie here. EVERYONE works hard, but I have special respect for the nurses and doctors who come in close contact with the patients, love on them and treat them.

A Doctor's perspective (Dr. Mark Agness):

"Carry each other's burdens, and in this way you will fulfill the law of Christ." - Galatians 6:2 (NIV)

As I fumble my way through the Italian chart of a patient admitted to our ICU, I look for the common kernels of information contained in all medical charts. With the help of interpreters and the sense of general similarities in the Italian and American "medicalese", I gaze at the minimally responsive intubated patient on the bed under the fluorescent lights and wonder about her family, occupation, passions, beliefs, and personality quirks. The record doesn't provide answers. She is an Italian woman of 62 years of age from the region of Cremona with a past history of high blood pressure and diabetes. That's it. Even a call to family through the interpreter adds little to my understanding of this human being lying quietly in the bed. She could be an American woman. She could be from my hometown with similar interests and background, a mother, or a fan of Celtic music like me. That's the point I guess. She is a "sister" made in the image of God with a rich past that I can scarcely imagine.

As we allow her to awaken, I try to empathize. When she was last awake, she was ill in her local hospital under the care of Italian physicians. She may have been aware she was not doing very well and that her shortness of breath was not improving. She might have been told that she would require intubation and the help of a breathing machine. Now, as she awakens from a drug induced coma, she has a tube in her throat. She is unable to speak and this is clearly not the same place she last remembers. She is in a tent surrounded by people she doesn't recognize speaking a language not her own.

Moreover, she is extremely weak. She has a catheter in her bladder, tube from nose to stomach, and requires the help of nursing staff to turn her regularly to prevent bed sores. The feelings of isolation and helplessness must be profound. The fear and confusion, tremendous. And there is no family. One of the cruel realities of the COVID outbreak is the "no visitation" policy both at our RCU as well as at the local hospital. No one can visit their loved ones, even in the throes of death. No one.

And yet, there is a common brotherhood. Nurses, physicians, and patients. All trying to establish a human connection. We speak to our patients knowing they probably don't understand what we're saying. We have interpreters speak to them even when it seems unlikely they are alert enough to comprehend the nuances of conversational speech. We touch our patients, hold hands, comb their hair, brush their teeth, and as if we can pray with them and over them. We play music, dim the lights at night, and try to allow family to communicate with them by holding a cell phone to their ears. We know little about them, other than what we learn from the chart and ongoing testing, yet we come to love them.

On the occasion of a response - a squeeze of the hand or followed command, we celebrate and share our successes. "Mrs. Z opened her eyes!" "Mr P squeezed my hand when the interpreter talked to him!"

I think the patients appreciate our excitement. Each small success is a potential step toward separation from the mechanical ventilator and discharge from the ICU. The bond between patient and primary nurse is particularly special. The analogy of family is really not a stretch. The nurses talk about their patients off shift, over dinner, recounting progress...or decline. They become attached. They celebrate successes, mourn failures, and we all mourn death.

Death in the RCU is inevitable. Our patients are clinging to life on arrival. The survival rate of COVID patients on ventilators is abysmal. Try as we might, using all that we know about ventilator management, prevention of complications, and management of the Coronavirus, we fail and some of the patients decline. The frustrating thing is that there seems to be no clear predictor of which patients will rally and improve and which will decline. It leaves us asking answerless questions about how we could have changed management or improved care. We have a "no code" policy. As patients fail, we choose not to do chest compressions. The reason for this is simple. The chance of "success" defined by a return to their current state is low and the risk to staff by spreading the aerosolized virus particles is great. In a "do no harm" world, a cardiac code doesn't make sense.

Yet it's not all grim by any means. Our patients wake up and begin to interact even while intubated. The bonds between provider and patient grow as these interactions become more complex. "No more pasta or gelato!" is the advice given to a portly, alert patient with whom the nurse has developed a maternal relationship. The response is a chuckle and grin. I suspect the patient has heard this advice before from another concerned female family member. We later learn this patient makes Cannoli for a living.

Another patient who is very much awake and anxious responds wonderfully to the simple touch of a hand. Between the nurse and me, we sit at her bedside, simply holding the patient's hand for hours, helping her to relax and sleep. We later learn she is a retired nurse at the local hospital. She has a much deeper familiarity with her environment and medical interventions than others. Her anxiety is easier to understand. The language and cultural barriers between patient and provider are largely erased. We are fellow humans. We are neighbors. We share our anxieties and needs wordlessly.

The parable of the Good Samaritan in the gospel of Luke is a remarkable piece of reasoning and rhetoric. We sometimes lose sight of the importance of the context of Jesus' parable. We learn that the parable was told in response to a question posed by a teacher of Jewish law, "...what must I do to inherit eternal life?" The teacher of the law answered wisely quoting the Shema written in Deuteronomy 6:8, but added something very interesting which wasn't found in Deuteronomy; namely, "…love your neighbor as yourself." Leviticus 19:18 (NIV) Good answer. Jesus subsequently ties this answer regarding the vitality of our spiritual life to the understanding of loving our neighbors. It's not about what you say, it's about what you do with your knowledge.

Why did SP respond to Italy? After all, Italy is a part of the EU. Shouldn't that massive institution provide for its own? For that matter, why would SP respond to NYC? As a faith-based organization, SP is despised by the intellectual leadership of one of the most secular cities in the world. The answer obviously lies in the simplicity of Jesus' parable. Jesus doesn't tell us who the man was who was beaten, robbed, and left for dead. We don't know if he was a foreigner, a pauper, a thief, or a nobleman. We don't have any insight into his spiritual state, beliefs, or past behaviors. We know nothing about him, and that's the point. This blank slate, this Everyman, is our neighbor and it matters not in the least what his "particulars" are. The same is true for Italy and NYC. SP responds because the gospel and NT in general is a call to action and the call couldn't be any clearer than the parable of the Good Samaritan.

Yet, I remember the reason Jesus gave us the parable and try to understand it in the context of the COVID pandemic. Our patients and their families understand better than most the frailty of human life, the helplessness of an isolating illness, and the very real spiritual crisis that ensues. Is there anything beyond this life? Can our cultural paradigm of bad luck, bad karma, and bad hygiene really be the only explanation given for this catastrophe? Is there a more personal, spiritual lesson to be learned? The volunteers from SP obviously think so and are willing to "risk" their health to bring this message to our brothers and sisters, our neighbors in Italy and NYC. There is life beyond our biology and physiology and dignity that reflects the very nature of a caring God. Responding to Italy is not an option, it's a mandate.

7 BROKENNESS

March 30, 2020

I was talking with Dr. Barb Zimmerman, who I roomed with our first night in North Carolina. Dr. Barb and I enjoyed each other's company but our workplaces and schedules put us where we didn't get to interact as much while in Italy! When we did see each other, we were both commenting how we felt like we were in a dream…(not exactly a good dream either) and another coworker, Regina Randolph, said it feels like we are in a sci-fi movie.

By 3PM, it's a little quiet for me. I'm not complaining! You know I like to be busy! The nurses and docs are busy all the time. It's surprisingly normal here… in a way. In the ICU are the sickest, and one of our ICU patients was moved to a stepdown ward, which means he may be recovering! That is a MIRACLE! He called his nurses "his angels". And believe me, he meant it. I never knew to the extent of what these nurses do. They do everything. And I mean EVERY conceivable thing you can think of. They are amazing. Those who are not the sickest are in the stepdown men or women's wards. The patients get bored and I don't blame them. You can't see company or family. No television. Not even anything to read. We are considered in the "hot" zone, so whatever you bring in here CANNOT go back out. A book, knitting? Anything! They are bored and I am sure when they are released to go home, they are sooo happy! I will say the nurses do everything they can to accommodate and bring smiles to the patients!

SP is deploying a new team to Manhattan… probably setting up tents in Central Park! That will also be tough because it is still winter there! Thankfully they found two med techs to cover for Manhattan. That is so great! I hate to leave here… but I knew I could commit to the 4 weeks and that was tough enough to be away from my loved ones during this crisis. I am thankful I came but it is hard… and hard is relative. To Kelly Sites, who served with Dr. Kent Brantley during the Ebola crisis, THAT would be considered hard to them… and perhaps this is considered easier in comparison (I mean we ARE having marvelous hot showers and sleep in a real bed with real food made by a Chef!). So, comparatively, this is a breeze. But I guess no matter what, deploying away from your family for so long, your schedule drastically changing… 12-13 hour days or long days and on call at night… all of this is not easy. Being in this hot, uncomfortable personal protective gear is not fun… but it certainly reminds me of how HARD our military has had it (there is not even a comparison there!) and how hard welders (like my brother & nephew) and constructions workers in their gear have had to work! After deployments like this, I go home extremely grateful! Speaking of home, I'm wondering how they will pull things off to get us home. I heard we may fly into Washington, DC and go home from there. Time will tell!

The afternoon and evening brought patients being released! What a wonderful thing! Their oxygen level has to be 94% or above. A new treatment that was recommended was Acetic Acid treatments (vinegar). One of the doctors (Dr. Bob Spencer) said to me in a lighthearted way, "Gargle with vinegar"! Well, they have balsamic vinegar and olive oil here, so I'll be enjoying that every evening. Can't hurt!

It is so encouraging to see some of the patients getting released! To even see an ICU patient get out and into a stepdown ward! That is truly amazing! Can you tell I am feeling encouraged?

Spring is coming here, with some beautiful days in the 50s and 60s. I'm enjoying the cool day weather and I'm not currently working nights (but will be trading off soon!), but I doooo look forward to the beaches with my husband! I have heard the public beaches are closed in my hometown. I wonder if we can ride our bikes and manage some beach time when I get home? We'll see! (**Post-deployment**: We all were required to be quarantined for two weeks.)

I was thinking that if each nurse, doctor, or technologist added up their time in a mask, goggles, face-shield, gloves, etc., it would be a total of 15 collective days of wearing this stuff during a 30-day deployment. I might be dreaming of donning (putting PPE on) and doffing (taking PPE off) for a long time!

I have never before found such solace in the Bible. It seems like there is a verse that covers just about everything. It's been winter here. Our first few days were ICE cold, blowing wind. We had no coats, no warm clothes (mainly just light jackets, but were not prepared for the bitter weather). We had to "don" our PPEs on in the blowing wind (20° Fahrenheit weather) and doff them in the same weather! We later got coats, thanks to Samaritan's Purse putting out the alarm. Now Spring is showing up… some light rains. Still cold but warmer weather in the day. The trees are budding and even patients are able to get out of their hospital beds here at the Samaritan's Purse hospital and sit outside in a chair or wheelchair! ANOTHER man is off the ventilator in the ICU! Truly a miracle!

My verse for today is Song of Songs 2:11-13 (NIV) – "See! The Winter is past; the rains are over and gone. Flowers appear on the earth; the season of singing has come, the cooing of doves is heard in our land. The fig tree forms its early fruit; the blossoming vines spread their fragrance. Arise, come, my darling; my beautiful one, come with me."

For my darling husband:

So, fun stuff. I am playing your worship music in my tent! So your music is playing here in Italy, ministering to the sick and to those of us who are working! I am tired as the day gets closer to quitting time. Really tired. It is 5:30PM here and that means it's 12:30PM there. How is the weather? How are you doing? How is your Mom? Please wear your mask when visiting her. This is taking the elderly out and even people your and my age. Crazy! I sure miss you! I leave the tent grounds around 6:45 or 7PM, so around 2:00PM your time, that's when you can say, "Yay, my wife made it another day!" I can't wait to be home. I feel like I'm in a dream for sure. I kept saying, I can make it to my 1st Friday… and then I can make it to April 1st. Then I will shoot for April 9th! And then April 18th! "Please, Lord, bless me with continued health and stamina!" I am doing amazingly well. Honestly, the hardest thing really is wearing this PPE all day. Can't wait to be home. I love you honey. Write me some news! How is Elijah paying his bills? How is Canaan's job? So glad Alli is okay. Hope Nate is well. Love you!

March 31, 2020

With New York having such high numbers of COVID, the peak will not be for 14-21 days, according to the latest statistics. US cases today are at 164K with 3,170 deaths and 5,507 recovered. Daily new cases for the US are at 20K right now. US deaths ten days ago were at 301. They have escalated to 3,170 in ten days. Just saw on the news, the police in Chicago dispersed an elderly crowd gathered at an Assyrian Church for a funeral. How terrible! Also, Washington, DC is at the same numbers that NY was at several weeks ago. Because the US is so large, short of a miracle, this could spring up in pockets all over the US.

Italy has surpassed 100K Coronavirus cases. Because it is a country comparable in size to California and this is all contained in the country, they are taking a hard toll, but they will also be over it the quickest. Can you imagine that this all started just 6 weeks ago for them? Today is the first day I've seen deaths go DOWN in Italy by 1%. It is currently all those cases that have an outcome; discharges are at 56% and deaths at 44%. Daily new cases in Italy are at 4,050! The new case curve seems to be going down. That is the lowest drop since March 18th; however, deaths were at 812 yesterday. Every day I hear the sirens in this Lombardy region of Italy. Every day, I hear multiple sirens.

That means a new case. An EMT in our crew (Mark) who is from Tennessee, just found out his Aunt is on a ventilator and his Uncle has a fever. Both tested positive for COVID.

Make a chart and see if there is any change. The incubation period is 2-14 days after being exposed. There are outlying days. Then a cough, flulike symptoms and shortness of breath. This virus moves so quickly and you can go from feeling slightly bad to a ventilator within 14 days. There is a positive; eighty percent of all cases are mild. And of course, these numbers are really the best that we can estimate, because all positive COVID's should be reported and that is how we get any statistic. If you have pre-existing conditions, this puts you at a total higher risk. So, if you are around your elderly/older parents or neighbors, you could carry it and infect someone very easily. Also, otherwise healthy people do seem to develop pneumonia after contracting the virus.

Gosh, this must all sound so grim…and it is for the families who have their loved one on the ventilator, or the family member that dies suddenly. I feel a little like I'm in a sci-fi movie, moving around in these gowns, face-shields, goggles, facemasks… It is dreamlike, not exactly a good dream. One thing that has shone more than anything, is the sureness of Jesus and the sureness of heaven. THAT one thing. That is everything. Samaritan's Purse understands the theology of suffering. There IS suffering in the world. Good and godly people can die and do. There is a fine line between FAITH in Christ and FAITH that nothing bad will happen to you. Sometimes BAD things happen to the best and brightest of His servants! THAT is true. No matter what happens in this life, GOD is faithful to walk us through it!

And now, the happy stuff. Cappuccino in the mornings, around 10:30AM. Someone brought over like 10 "Easter" Cakes, made with dried oranges and almonds. The Italian's love language IS food. Amazing. I walked over to the admin tent and there were homemade pizzas galore! Every kind you could imagine! I opted out of those because that will put me to sleep! We were also sent some blueberries, strawberries and pineapple, and lunch has been sent over, though I'll wait another hour before I go over! It's VERY cold again today, 6°C (42.8°F). And windy! It was rainy through the night. Barb, my partner, has worked the night shift since I've been here. I'm not my sharpest at night, but I'm hoping we can trade shifts soon, because she is older than me and must be exhausted! Looking at the weather as best I can, it appears it may get cold again tonight (32°F). I am worried for her. I wish I had the stamina to work longer hours, but by 6:45PM, I am wiped out. We will figure out how to switch shifts. Please pray she and I will have the stamina to keep going. It's a marathon, not a sprint. Thanking God that He made me to be a marathoner (I was never good at sprinting!)

On another note, I really, really miss home. I cannot think about it much, or I'll have a panic attack or something. I just miss home. I miss my husband. I miss our tiny condo. I miss the beach. I miss the sunshine. I miss simplicity. I'm not complaining, just miss everyone. This time will be behind me soon enough, but I KNOW God brought me here.

To my darling husband:

It seems like every afternoon around 4PM, I am close to having a bit of a panic attack. And by that I don't mean afraid of COVID. Just a feeling that I want to be home and can I do this? I guess I have felt this way every trip I've taken, but when you are wearing PPEs for so long, it gets confining. It's been a cold, rainy, yucky day. But I think it must have been terrible for my coworker, Barb, last night! I asked if the crew could make this tent warmer for Barb at night, because it will get cold again tonight, and they brought five heaters! So, that's awesome! When I get discouraged and want to come home, I start reading scriptures and it REALLY helps me. I know people are praying and that is giving me strength. My scriptures today are:

2 Corinthians 4:17 "For our light and momentary troubles are achieving for us an eternal glory that far outweighs them all." (NIV)

Exodus 33:14 "The Lord replied, 'My presence will go with you, and I will give you rest.'" (NIV)

And lastly Psalms 16:8 "I have set the Lord always before me, because He is at my right hand, I will not be shaken." (ESV) I love you forever, my love, and tomorrow is April 1st!

God is breaking me in a way of sorts. My heart is breaking. My spirit is breaking…my physical body is tired. Hardship brings one closer to God, and THAT is the most beautiful thing about hardship. Our team has been treated so well. Like royalty really. We have three amazing meals a day, coffee, hot showers, and a comfy bed to sleep in. There is just something about sickness all around you, realizing that you are a breath away from eternity, that bring you even closer to God. I can't wait for that day, and yet, I don't want to leave this earth yet. I feel I have more to do. I want to make an impression on my grandchildren now and the ones yet to be born. I want more time with my husband and time with my family. This earth is fleeting fast. There is nothing more than I want in my life, than Christ, the BEST thing that ever happened to me. How He found me! "Oh, blessed Father, how good You are to me! Let me be a willing vessel to serve You! Let me be a blessing to all I come in contact with!"

A Nurse's Perspective (Taylor Pitkin):

One story I will share is about a patient who came to us early on in the month with a chronic trach. He was admitted to the male ward in which I was working at the time. He presented like someone who would overcome the virus after a few days of supportive care. No one anticipated that his viral secretions would become too thick to manage, leading to the inability to clear them and ultimately to infection that his body just could not overcome. Very quickly he became weak and lost the ability to perform selfcare, and in order to keep his airway open we had to frequently suction out his trach with a catheter that went down into his lungs. This procedure was extremely painful for him to undergo, but out of necessity it started happening at more frequent intervals. I came to dread the times that I was the one inflicting the pain on him.

The night nurse that I would hand off report to, came to me one evening crying, exclaiming "What can we do for him? I can't take it anymore." We starting praying over him before we would suction him, and though the peace of Jesus was tangibly present, this man was still suffering. The nights before he died, we surrounded his beside and sang hymns, praying for Jesus' comfort and sovereignty. I was asked for transfer units and start working in the ICU, so I didn't get to continue working directly with him, but my coworkers kept me updated on his condition each night. They made it a priority to ensure that someone was sitting with him at all times and had the opportunity to share the gospel with him over the course of the last days of his life. The translator read to him from Ephesians out of the Italian Bible and they continued to sing hymns because his body would oxygenate better as he relaxed to the sound of Jesus. He accepted Christ as his Savior before he died and entered into the gates of heaven surrounded by two nurses and the doctor singing him right into Jesus' arms.

"And the prayer offered in faith will make the sick person well; the Lord will raise them up. If they have sinned, they will be forgiven." James 5:15 (NIV)

A Doctor's Perspective (Dr. Mark Agness):

"Jesus wept." John 11:35 (NIV)

It was hard. This was my first deployment with a DART through Samaritan's Purse. Not so for many of my teammates who had deployed elsewhere to places like the Bahamas, Mozambique, Iraq. In fact, Sasha Thew, one of my ICU nurses, had deployed twice to the DRC to respond to the Ebola outbreak. All of my colleagues had other jobs, careers, and commitments. Many of the nurses worked "per diem" or "casual" as the Canadians put it. Essentially working as needed without a schedule, allowing them to respond at the drop of a hat to disasters worldwide. Some were retired and volunteering their time like my physician colleagues Barb, Bob, Julie and Paul. All were used to hard work, sleep deprivation, and stress.

Each DART, I am told, is unique. This response to Italy (and NY) were the first to developed nations. This DART, as I later learned, was unique because SP didn't know how they might get us home. Travel had been disrupted and borders closed. The travel situation changed daily and our planned return tickets were a matter of wishful thinking than true reservations. This DART would require wearing PPE for long periods. Though much hotter and more restrictive, the PPE for Ebola was worn for a maximum of two hours (reflecting the risk of dehydration and hyperthermia). We would wear PPE for twelve hour stretches.

Had I been asked if I was physically able to work twelve-hour shifts for 28 to 30 days, at night, in PPE, in an ICU - I would probably have replied "no". The spirit was willing but the body weak. I'm sixty years old. Fatigue was a given. I became tired physically as I anticipated twelve hours in the ICU standing in mud boots in PPE. I became tired emotionally trying to make hard decisions, watching patients suffer and die. I became tired spiritually, trying to make sense of this experience in the lives of my patients, their families, and my staff. We all struggled at some time and responded in various ways.

We exercised as we were able. It seemed a good way to manage stress. Prior to a night shift, I ran the stairs at the hotel as did several others. We did pushups, dips, sit-ups, and various other low-resource exercises. We read, prayed, ate, and supported each other. Meals were a time to interact normally. They were loud and sometimes boisterous. We told jokes – lousy jokes, but nevertheless helping to lighten the mood. One ICU nurse, Josh Verner, came from a long line of jokesters and took great joy in telling "dad" jokes (and luring the gullible) – you know the kind - "Why did the chicken cross the road?..." I later decided his mother must be a saint to put up with this over the course of years. We played practical jokes on one another. We posted humor on the group app, "WhatsApp". Quarantine pickup lines were a favorite.

We held contests in the ICU. Using a walker, we announced a "dip" contest over the camp radio one night. Several came from the wards to the ICU to see how many dips could be done in a minute (Ian and Josh were in a virtual tie – my effort was less but recorded for posterity to prove even the ancients were game). We announced and began 5AM yoga in the ICU led by nurse Grace Chase. I still smile at photos of graceful nurses in graceless PPE striking poses. Similar events occurred on the wards.

In all, we became masters at managing our stress and dealing with the chaos that surrounded us. We clung to the normal rhythms of life, distracted ourselves with humor, built relationships, and leaned...no, clung to God who enabled us. Twelve-hour shifts for 28 days? It really wasn't a problem. Life became simple.

Guys don't like to talk about crying any more than they like to ask directions. I'm no different, but it wouldn't be honest if I didn't confess that I wept. I teared up on several occasions, both happy and sad. I worried about decisions and their consequences. I frequently wondered what I or we could have done better. One death stands out to me. We received a ventilated patient from the hospital. He was young in his 50s. He had been ventilated, extubated, and seemed to have been recovering at the hospital. The morning of the transfer he had taken a turn for the worse and required reintubation. On arrival he was very sedated as were most of our patients. Other than a rapid heart rate, there seemed little difference from our other patients. He arrived with a pile of papers that comprised his medical record.

Within twenty minutes of arrival, his oxygen-need increased and blood pressure dropped. Within 5 minutes he was in full cardiopulmonary arrest. Because of his age and suddenness of the change, I chose to break protocol and perform a "code" with chest compressions. I didn't understand what was happening initially. An emergency X-ray was OK. An EKG showed diffuse changes suggesting damage to heart muscle. Despite multiple, brief return to spontaneous circulation in response to compressions and medications, he continued to decline. Ultimately, we had to stop the effort and allow him to die. In likelihood he threw a clot to his lungs precipitated by the transport and transfer to our ICU. We later came to learn that this virus increased the risk of these events. I didn't know this at the time.

One of the horrible consequences of the death of a patient is informing the family. It was always unclear how much the family knew of the illness or the patient's course. The patient's care had originated elsewhere and contact with the family was limited in our situation. The Italian medical culture differs from ours with regard to informing families and involving them in decision making. We struggled with this fact frequently. Generally, in Italy the physicians made the decisions and subsequently shared them with patient and family. In America, we consult family and involve them in the process throughout the course of care. Calling a family "cold" from Ospedale (Hospital) Americano through an interpreter was challenging for all. The interpreters realize these conversations will be hard and emotional. Several quit because of this.

The family was completely unprepared for the news and their response reflected it. The wailing from multiple voices was heartbreaking. Between tears, we tried to explain what had happened. Both the interpreter and I struggled with this conversation. The family hadn't seen their husband/father/son for weeks and now learned he had died in the company of strangers. How do we make this better? How can we even begin to comfort, much less begin the process of healthy grieving? I had no answers them and have none now. I wept.

Though I focus on a single death here, it's hard not to emphasize the ripple effect of this death and the thousands of others brought on by COVID-19. Each patient is a father/mother/brother/sister, spouse, co-worker, friend. Each patient leaves a legacy, memories, and unfinished business. Each was a child of God with a soul. Multiply this by thousands and I began to understand the devastation and sorrow. This type of tragedy is not unique to Italy nor to Coronavirus, of course. This country has lived through wars, the plague, influenza, and multiple tragedies. The world today struggles with famine, civil war, terrorism, genocide, and brutal persecution. So, it's not unique to this situation or time but each life is unique, special and known to its Maker.

The process of empathy can be both overwhelming and overwhelmed. As someone close to us suffers, the pain is intense, personal and palpable. As we are subject to multiple tragedies, that ability to feel empathetically can be overwhelmed. Our emotional response seems inadequate and we start to wonder if we have developed a "callousness" or inability to care and feel. It certainly happens in medicine, war, and disaster. It encourages me that, as anonymous as tragedy and death can become in our instant media world, Jesus is able to feel and weep for one man. In fact, He is able to feel and weep for each of us. There is no limit to His empathy and no life or soul unknown to Him.

8 YOU SHALL LIVE

April 1, 2020

Every morning, I hop out of bed at 5:45AM in the morning, brush my teeth (I've already showered the evening before), put on my baggy scrubs, because the hospital here in Cremona graciously loaned us some! Grab my backpack and run down three flights of stairs. Then a quick breakfast! I get hot tea every morning (Earl Grey, thinking of you, Paul!). As you know I don't drink hot tea at home, but there's a lot I have done here that I don't do at home! Breakfast is always about the same. You can choose from scrambled eggs, hardboiled egg, bran cereals, fruit (oranges, apples, pineapples and PRUNES), a variety of ITALIAN cheeses that are out of this world, some hard, prepackaged toast… delicious and various deli-type meats. I usually have a little of everything, except the meat. So, the food is truly amazing here. Then we have announcements and a quick devotional, and then "back to the bus, back to the bus." Sounds like a good beginning to a rap song. Always reminders to not get lazy on washing hands and wearing our PPEs very carefully. Every morning I get to the lab and see what order of business is next. I clean up also, using 0.5% chlorine to wipe everything down. And I mean everything. Chairs, tent door flaps, phones, radios, pens… anything that you might touch. So, once all is clean, it's order of business in the lab, just like any laboratory job.

This morning, I heard on the radio that one of our patients died. You get used to their names, used to seeing them… and it's sad. However, there are AMAZING triumphs in the ICU and we discharge patients daily! Lots of them! That part is so encouraging! But it's a reminder of the losses… who are real people… whose family loves them. There is a couple working so hard here with SP (Mark & Regina Randolph). They live in Crossville, Tennessee. As of yesterday, there were 17 people in their county who were diagnosed with COVID. Mark's Aunt

& Uncle were two of them. It is such a reminder to be diligent not to be around our older loved ones and to be diligent to wear a mask if we are. They are the more fragile and the ones who typically get sick.

Okay, on a practical note, when you wear these masks for such long hours, you develop a calloused nose. All of our noses are red and sore. Don't judge, but it may alter my nose permanently. I hope not. (Smile.) Another wonderful thing - Michael W. Smith put out an Italian version of the song "Waymaker" by Sinach. It is so beautiful! Makes me want to cry every time I hear it! Also, Rick & Canaan's music on Spotify, I have been playing throughout the day. It brings me closer to home and I am loving it!

I'll finish this note with a scripture. 2 Timothy 2:11 "Here is a trustworthy saying: If we died with him, we shall also live with him." (NIV)

For the second day in a row, new cases have fallen to 4,000 here in Italy; however, daily deaths are still up at 837 and one was lost here at our SP hospital today. There is only ONE HOPE for all of us. It is our HOPE in Jesus Christ. He never lets us down. He walks with us in the loneliest of times, in the darkest of hours. We WILL feel sadness and loss in this world. It is a given, until His coming. Lord Jesus, come quickly. And I say that, Lord, come quickly…in our darkest of hours… in our saddest of times. Be with those who have lost loved ones. Be near us. Amen

Today, April 1, 2020, US Coronavirus cases are at 188K. Four-thousand deaths…and seven-thousand recovered. My eyes are on Florida, Texas, Colorado, Oklahoma, Missouri, and Germany… where my immediate family is. Lord, may your hand ever be with us in times of trouble. Talking with my husband last night, and of course, no one knows the future but financially there is bound to be a tremendous reaction (for every action, there is an equal and opposite reaction) and the domino effect of restaurants being out of business…this affects ability to pay mortgages and rents. I remember very clearly my Grandparents talking about the stock market crash of 1929 and how foods were rationed and how very difficult times were. For nearly 100 years, we have known prosperity. Could those times be coming to an end? Is this the generation that will know some suffering in America? Lord, only Your hands can save us all.

I made it to April 1st! I'll be saying that all day! I can't say it loud enough. It's hard to be in this PPE for 12 hours a day, every day, seven days a week… but the NURSES and DOCTORS, they are heroes!! They do heavy lifting of patients… they clean their ventilators… they clean their bodily fluids. They do the hardest jobs! That is not to overshadow the other teams, who provide our water and set up the tents and do the logistics that are so necessary! But these nurses and doctors will have a special crown to give to Jesus, of that I am sure! I think it might be the Coronavirus Crown! That sounds funny, but can you imagine? They probably take the biggest risks, as their patients are so sick and they are in tents where there is much coughing. They are FEARLESS (though in the quiet moments of making it back to the hotel, I am sure FEAR raises its ugly head!) Fear of this terrible virus. And they have a right to fear something that can take their lives. THEY are on the frontlines of this battle. I pray that those who are safe inside their homes will pray for them! Many of these nurses are young women, with futures ahead of them. They dream of marriage and children someday. Some of the nurses are mothers of adult kids and have spouses. Some of them are daughters, sons, and siblings. And some are at the highest risk because of age. We all have family to go home to. I spoke with translator Antonio Marino (who is a pastor in Italy) and he spoke with some of the patients. They cannot believe the compassion and love that our nurses and doctors exhibit. Some patients remarked that they couldn't tell the difference between the doctors or the nurses, because of how beautifully they interacted with each other. How our nurses and doctors pray together! I wish I could encourage my US friends who are believers, to be courageous and pray at their public institutions. I see how prayer is giving STRENGTH to the weak (medical personnel and patients). I thank God it is sunny outside today. We saw another patient leave this place to go to his home! And we all stood outside and clapped.

I just saw a man who was on a ventilator and now he is OFF! He is walking with a walker and trying to walk a few steps! Of course, he reminds me of my dad and I find myself emotional. But these people are so grateful. When you are THAT close to death and God has given you more time with family, you are elated and filled with joy. Your heart is so tender towards God. So here is the scripture that I found that seems to fit these moments so perfectly. My last verse of the night.

Ezekiel 37:5-6 "Thus says the Lord God to these bones: Behold, I will cause breath to enter you, and you shall live. And I will lay sinews upon you, and will cause flesh to come upon you, and cover you with skin, and put breath in you, and you shall live, and you shall know that I am the LORD." (ESV)

April 2, 2020

I made it thus far! I know it seems petty, but each day is rather long… and at 57 years old, my stamina would normally be limited. God TRULY is making this happen because I can say unequivocally, that it is not my strength.

We had an announcement that a nurse from Cremona Hospital, who works with us, tested positive for COVID. It is all around us. So, Lord, once again, I ask for Your protection… and like Shadrach, Meshach and Abednego said, "Our God is able to deliver us, but even if He does not, we will still serve Him" (my sloppy paraphrase) Daniel 3:17-18. And, yes, I am taking every precaution there is. Trust Jesus…trust the science. Lord, Bless me with health. Bless me with a strong immune system to fight off this terrible virus! And now, I sure hate to keep giving statistics…but Italy's cases are up to 110K. Daily cases went up 700 patients yesterday to 4700 cases…after a two day drop to 4000. Deaths went DOWN to 727 from 837 the day before. There is a very small downward trend. Still the outcome ratio is 56% recovered/discharged to 44% deaths.

The US statistics made a jump from 188K yesterday to 215K (NY and NJ bearing the brunt of this with 105K of those numbers); however, Florida has gone up to 7773 cases. Let's remember that New York had 8,300 cases on March 20th…just two weeks ago. (At the time of this printing June 6, 2020 - NY had 376K confirmed cases with 24,175 deaths and 66,756 currently recovered. New York peaked in mid-April and the trend has been steadily going down.) At that rate, Florida and other states could experience those same numbers. (At the time of printing June 6, 2020, Florida DID NOT experience those same numbers; however, the country is still in a battle with coronavirus. By June 17, 2020 the Florida numbers were ramping up.) What is truly scary is that NY is only 5 weeks into this virus (from the very 1st case) and it may not be long before it surpasses the entire country of Italy in statistics. New York cases are steadily rising, exponentially. I can't express enough how important it is to wash your hands, your face, your neck if you are out (wear a mask if you have one), and please don't be around the medically compromised…or older population.

I feel like I report so much of the grim statistics. I want to report good stuff too. The sun is shining here in the Lombardy region of Italy! It is a beautiful day! It is cold… around 1°C (33.8°C); however, there is no wind and it is a perfect day! The Samaritan's Purse New York tents are up and they are receiving their first patients.

We are discharging many patients a day from the regular wards! Each one who comes out get a round of applause! And some of the ICU patients who were on death's door, are OFF the ventilators and are walking with walkers! I have never witnessed so much love from a team before! Please pray with me that their health will remain strong. One older man came out for his first walk on his walker and everyone clapped. He started blowing kisses to everyone!

Today is a new day. A new day of miracles and I am praying for continued stamina for myself and for our team. I will likely start night shift soon, so please pray for me on that one. Barb, my coworker is older than me and she needs some serious rest. God willing, Barb can get some very much needed rest. I plan to take the night shift from 7PM to 7AM. Pray I can sleep. Pray I have stamina and pray I can visually see (you know I am pretty much night blind now. 😊 So LOTS to pray about!

I wish you all could see what a beautiful day it is today, and I wish I could take photos of the four women patients (all Italian) who are enjoying a picnic lunch outside the tent! It's fantastic! The sun is shining and it is beautiful, chilly weather. With them enjoying the weather, I have no doubts they will be going home soon. Some of these patients have been in the hospital for 6 weeks! These ladies are singing and laughing! I will see this picture in my mind my whole life. It's a memory I wish I could capture by photograph and share with you, but we have to protect identities, of course, just like in the US. And this weather…it is so nice! It is actually like a perfect Tennessee day. The sun is shining and it's really, really cold (33 degrees Fahrenheit). It makes me think of the mountains and hiking on a perfect day. I do so look forward to home. My spirits are up, as it is April 2nd and tomorrow will be my halfway point.

A Nurse's Perspective (Taylor Pitkin):

Our translators were witnessed to as we asked them to be our voices to the patients. As a translator read from Ephesians, he exclaimed, "Wow, the bible really says that?" Opportunities to witness to patients and those with whom we were working were not ignored. They were the rhythms of our time there. A world searching for hope in the midst of fear is hearing about the Ultimate Healer and where our hope lies. A friend of mine wrote recently that the gospel has a way of spreading in oppositional circumstances.

"When it doesn't make sense for the Word of God to spread, it does anyway. Take persecution and martyrdom for example. In the same way, the Word of the Lord will continue to spread against all odds brought on by coronavirus. When the world is quarantined, the gospel is not. Though the world is at a standstill, the gospel is on the move."
~Ashli Roussel

9 MADE STRONG IN OUR WEAKNESS

April 3, 2020

The days are going much faster! I actually feel pretty good. Amazing! It is 2:15PM and I've been at work since 7AM. I will be working for another 11 hours, so an 18-hour day. Wow! I hope I feel as good at 1AM as I do now! So, Barb (my lab partner) and I are trading shifts. I am easing into 18 hours tonight and she will do 18 hours tomorrow and then we will both be doing separate shifts. The weather outside in Italy today is nothing short of gorgeous! I wish we could take a bit of time to see some of the city, but right now so many quarantined that we pretty much are resolved to be in the hotel and in the camp. Of course, on these deployments we come to work and there is never a thought that we can sightsee except our drive to and from work. So no expectations ever! This may be my only communication until 7PM tomorrow night, which is 2PM your time tomorrow. Not much else to say, except that this weather brings hope! Patients are sitting outside. Someone brought many flowers in pots to the camp and it is so beautiful to see color! We are used to white tents, gray buildings, yellow coats, and blue gloves. We look like something from outer-space. Well, I love you all and please tell everyone I won't be able to contact them for a day or longer.

Well, there is a possibility that I may get to head home around the 15th or 16th. I don't know. Either that or the 20th. We will see. At least I can make the 15th my new goal to get to! I'm sure that day will be here before I know it. The last four days have gone by very quickly. I don't know why, but they have. The weather has been so nice, it has really lifted my spirits. The numbers in Italy are just about staying the same. I don't hear ambulances nearly as much as I did, but I still hear them. This virus is incredible. It's amazing that it can invade and do the damage it does.

April 4, 2020

Well, it's a little past midnight and my night is going much faster than the days! It is busier and I can handle busy! I wanted to share a little of my day yesterday. I worked an 18-hour shift that I managed pretty well. I was certainly ready to make it back to the hotel (did I say "hotel")! We have a hotel and a comfortable bed! So, I got back around 1:30AM after having worked since 7AM the previous day. I took a shower and went right to sleep for 7 hours. I wish I could have slept more but I was grateful for that! I met a wonderful young EMT, Jake Chasteen, who had just come in from Boone, North Carolina. He was homeschooled and I enjoyed talking with him. He is a fine young man with an awesome future ahead of him! He plans to go to PA school at University of Florida. I had fun sharing the ins and outs of the lab and sharing our favorite books. His was the *Count of Monte Cristo*! Go figure! My favorite movie! Anyway, Jake had the day off and I had an "extra" 6 hours, so yesterday we walked to the only places we were allowed, which were the grocery store and pharmacy. The lines to both were too long. What a strange site. Seeing people in lines for hours to shop. It certainly is reminiscent of photos of the Depression, only this time the grocery stores have food and people are able to buy.

April 5, 2020

It is Sunday evening and I just started my 3rd late night shift. I think maybe I've been pampered all my life, because I've never worked a night shift. It has taken some getting used to, but because I have no family here, I feel I can do it and it is busier at night, so that makes the time pass quickly. I look at the date and I think I am well into April. My next mental goal is April 7th! I keep pushing that goal up. Somehow, goals help me. Hey guys, please send me a note if you read these updates. If they are boring you, it's okay, but it's encouraging to me to know someone is caring and reading what I and others are going through. I have never worked in a hospital setting (besides Ecuador) and that was an eye-opener. So, being in and out of the ICU and seeing what these nurses and doctors do, well, they are my superheroes forever more! I wish all of America could experience this and walk a mile in these PPEs. It IS hard, but I'm somewhat getting used to it. I heard this evening that the number of deaths are at the lowest they've been in a while in Italy. What HOPE! I do pray it continues this way. Epidemiologists are predicting that the US peak will be April 15th/16th. I don't know how this will play itself out in the US, as we are a large land-mass compared to Italy. I will look forward to having a time of rest at home in quarantine!

The weather here is warming up. In the daytime, the patients are able to get out of their hospital wards (tents) and sit outside on chairs. Someone brought pots of flowers to the camp and it has boosted all of us… the colors of Spring! At night, it still gets down to the 40s and remember - those who work at night - If they have to use the lavatory or get coffee, they doff all their PPEs off in the cold and run down the gauntlet we call "Main Street". We get our coffee or whatever and then run back in the cold to change into our PPEs again. The first two weeks were BITTER cold for the day and night shift. The tents blew so hard, you might have thought they would blow away. God bless that first wave night team… and my coworker, Barb, who bore the brunt of being the first team to come in. She took the night shift as well and is one of my all-time heroes. I'm in for a good night shift. It is a little quieter here until 10 or 11PM and then the night speeds forward with much to do. My body is not exactly strong and I've always dealt with pain and headaches much of my adult life. To be here, and not use Excedrin (aspirin and acetaminophen have been known to make Coronavirus worse) is really saying something. Once again, I believe only God's strength has made this possible. Dr. Mark Agness (from California) shared an amazing devotional of how all of us come with weaknesses, but God is made strong in our weakness. I am experiencing that 100% right now. Certainly, there are times I feel so lonely for home, or am beyond tired, but HE has given me strength.

Got to enjoy snapping a few photos of the square in Cremona (right in front of our hotel). There is a lovely cathedral nearby, but we don't have permission at this time to see it. Out of respect that the people are all quarantined, we are careful to only go where we are allowed. Today our first ICU patient walked out the door of the stepdown ward and got to go home! Imagine! Near death! Our nurses have used straws to help the people practice breathing exercises and balloons to exercise their lungs. We have had losses too, but miracles are happening. One Italian woman who is in one of our wards recovering, shared her story. It was heartbreaking. She spoke of feeling sick and her husband taking care of her. He took her to the hospital and waited until she got settled. While she was in the hospital, she tried in vain to reach him. When she couldn't get through on her calls, she asked the police to check on him. They had to break down the door of their home to check on him. He died the morning after he took her to the hospital. He had no symptoms (at least he didn't tell her). He was buried alone. And now she shares that she will say goodbye to him at the cemetery. I can't even imagine.

USA cases are close to 350K. Total deaths are 8,399 (879 cases per million population). New York and New Jersey take 147K of those numbers. New York with 3,500 deaths. Florida is now up to 11,545 confirmed cases. Italy cases confirmed are at 124K. The death rate has gone down one more percent to 42% of closed cases. That is encouraging. However, new cases are still at 4,500. The new cases curve appears to be going down. The deaths are still high, but that curve also seems to be going down. Spain is now in trouble with 126K cases.

10 THE BEST AND BRIGHTEST

Night of April 6, 2020

I have made it thus far. And, once again, only in God's strength. The night shift is moving quite a bit faster for me. I like to be busy and this is a busy time. No wonder hospitalized patients typically can't get much sleep.

I am encouraged. The numbers in Italy are slowly going down. The death rate is down the lowest in some time. The new cases are down, but not by a ton; however, they are down!

The people of Italy have showered us with welcome. With MUCH food, with encouragement! And our hotel! This has made the success of our deployment much more possible. With this virus, we might have been sleeping in the tents (with too many us, increasing the risk of COVID), taking showers in the cold, and maybe risk getting sick or more run down. The anonymous person who donated our hotel rooms and HIS chef, has been such a blessing to us. I have to say that being gone this long from family and working every day, repeating the same motions every day – it has been the RICH words of the Bible that has been our strength. We are super praying for New York. They have their jobs cut out for them. Unfortunately, they are being scrutinized. The people SP hire, are the BEST of the BEST. I say that unequivocally. I have never been with such giving, sacrificial, amazing people. I am more than humbled to be amongst them. What I find is that most of our older crew (the 50+) have physical ailments. We all hurt. Our bodies hurt. We can't always sleep like we want, and YET, our Father in heaven has brought us here and given us strength in our weakness. Some of the younger, amazing nurses also have their trials. They may be young, but some have autoimmune diseases and they serve in their weaknesses as well.

The first few teams are seeing the light at the end of the tunnel. Some are leaving I believe on April 10th and another group on April 14th. I have no idea yet when I am leaving. I think it will provide a sense of relief when I know. I am anxious to be with my family, though I will be quarantined for 14 days with just Rick & I. We will use that time to rest together. It will be hard because he cannot be around his mother, so I worry about that. I'm so grateful my sister Susan is with our mother right now and Rick's sister, Carla, can be with his mom. I won't worry that I will get them infected if I am carrying this virus.

Camp life has its groove now. No organization is perfect, but SP has done a remarkable job putting these camps up. They many times donate all the tents and supplies to the country they go to. It's truly amazing. When my kids were young, I cut out an article out of a women's magazine about being able to volunteer with the Red Cross during disasters. I tore it out (I still have it!) because I knew this was one of my great passions and I thought "one day, when my kids are grown and I am bored, I will do this!" The fact that I have had the opportunity to do this, now that my children have grown, is simply mind-boggling. I am so grateful to God that He gave me this opportunity.

I'm not accustomed to talking about negative things but for historic reasons, I am sharing statistics about this awful virus. The death rate of cases which had an outcome, has gone down to 42%. When I came here, it was 44%. New cases are at 4,316 and the curve is coming down. I pray with all my heart it stays that way. The lowest drop in deaths occurred last night with 525 deaths since March 20th, which had 627 deaths. This is so encouraging, though each life is a life with a story… and a life that creates a huge loss for someone when they die...

Sometimes I get weary of writing these statistics, but this is something none of us in our lifetime have experienced. Africa suffered with Ebola and most of us were far-removed from such awful tragedies. We Americans have been so blessed but this virus has stopped the world, including our safe and comfortable lives in the US. The total cases in the US have ramped up to 356,414. Total deaths 10,490. New York & New Jersey are 171K of that number. NY & NJ are at 5,700 deaths. Florida is up to 13,324 cases with 974 new cases today. I sure pray for all my family. I do wonder how this will continue to affect America. Will this spread? It's obviously all over the country. Will it go in waves with NY and NJ leading the way and the rest of America trailing? The total new cases have dropped considerably for the US - as of yesterday, down to 25,316. Is our curve coming down quicker?

Evening of April 7, 2020

It's the evening of April 7, 2020. I'll be working the night shift. It's tough when you're not used to it, but thankfully I am getting a bit more acclimated! It certainly has given me a fresh appreciation for those amazing souls who work the late-night hours. One thing I find is that I'm completely unsure of what day it is or what hour it is! And then when I finish the night shift, someone will say "Good Morning" and I find that somehow hysterical because I'm going to bed for the day!

Some of our ICU patients had a VERY rough night last night. Some are septic and some are just not improving. The nurses (and myself) get attached to seeing these patients survive, and so when a patient dies, we will never forget their names… and will always wonder about their stories. Sometimes I get calls from family… and I may already know they have passed away and their family does not know… and I have to maintain a professional calm. It's tough and again I have the utmost respect for the medical personnel that deal with this in their normal jobs at home as well. It IS the circle of life, but there is a reason why the Psalmist wrote (Psalm 23:4 KJV), "Yea, though I walk through the valley of the shadow of death, I will fear no evil," because death seems so final. For those who have found the Christ, our Holy Father, "Precious in the sight of the Lord is the death of his *faithful* servants." Psalm 116:5 (NIV) *Faithful.* That's what I want to be in all the world.

I have said this before, but Samaritan's Purse finds the best and brightest of servants. There is Josh Verner, who was a lifeguard and learned First Aid from some paramedics and then decided to become a nurse. Casey Diener from Denver, who is a nurse and has become passionate about finishing premed. Every evening and morning, Casey makes sure someone gives a devotional on the bus ride back to the hotel and it is there that I learn what amazing people I work with. The DEPTH of pain and suffering some have gone through. The love for Jesus and how they LOVE Him!

There is Mariah Bywater from South Carolina, who spent six years in China as a nurse. Taylor Pitkin, also a nurse from West Virginia (go Taylor! My roots state!), who spent nine months in Togo, Africa. Carolyn and Ian Larratt from Canada (a married couple) who spent a great deal of time serving in the Arctic and Alaska. Stephanie Morales, who is gorgeous at 38 years old, is a Physician's Assistant. Stephanie just finished two years of Bible School as well. She lost her dad young. There is just something about pain and suffering that gives you a depth and a greater love for the balm of Gilead.

Jim from Colorado, who spent 30+ years in the Army, also a Physician's Assistant with his Doctorate, who is serving! Dr. Julie McKay, a middle-aged energetic physician, whose daughter is serving in Switzerland. Julie has a light about her and shines with Jesus. There is also Dr. Kristin Hummel, who is in language school learning French, in order to serve in a hospital in Africa! Dr. Kristin spent some time in the Air Force and has a passion to be a surgeon! Claudia Evick is a nurse from West Virginia, middle-aged, and powers through aches and pains to do such a superb job!

Dr. Mark Agness, also middle-aged, powers through this deployment. Mark has two young adult sons and God is going to move mightily in their lives, I believe, just through their Dad's deployment and his willingness to put himself in harm's way! There is nurse Shannon Wood, who I adore! Shannon is the oldest in her family of four kids and she is a delight! Full of life, joy, and servanthood. She has a condition that causes her to have to take expensive medication monthly, but she keeps at it! She never stops! She too, has this most amazing soul. We lost our first patient, an older man, who was born the same year as my Dad. So, I would see him in the ICU and think "my Dad might have been this age," had he lived, (and of course, this thought filled me with sentiment) – and Shannon would love on him, taking care of him. Remember, no family can come here. They cannot see their loved ones. They are trusting in Samaritan's Purse to take care of them, as best we can. And when they die, their loved ones cannot see them. Well, we lost that patient and Shannon had grown attached (as do all the nurses and doctors, as they care for their patients). She had to come into my tent and have a good cry and then tend to the next patient. I had the honor of talking to the patient's daughter, who might well have been my age, and to say to her that her father had the BEST nurse, who took such good care of him.

And who can forget Kelly Arroyo from California! Kelly is also a middle-aged nurse and offered her wonderful, bright personality to pray with us morning and night!

Oh, and I don't want to forget Jake. Jake Chasteen is the 2nd son of four kids, living in Boone, North Carolina. He is currently a paramedic, but soon to take PA classes at University of Florida. He has such a fantastic personality and soaks up learning! Jake doesn't realize that his friendship really brightened my deployment. We had the same couple of hours off and Jake generously walked with me around the few places in Cremona we were allowed to go.

We have such a great team and I wish I could make mention of everyone! There were a large number of us and I so enjoyed getting to know everyone. Maybe as I go on, I can share about more about these great men and women of God.

And now some encouraging news. In Italy, cases that had an outcome – deaths have gone down to 41%! The CURVE is going down! Yesterday, our new cases were at 3,599. Deaths went up again but the trend seems to be going down. I think it's possible by middle of May,

Italy may possibly be over this.

US Statistics are faring better. Our cases which had an outcome means 21% deaths and 79% discharged/recovered. USA now has 386K cases with NY & NJ bearing 183K of those. For NY, 7,077 total cases per 1 million population and NJ 5,001 total cases per 1 million population. Florida is now at 14,504 cases with 283 deaths. I have looked at overall graphs and will probably do that when I get home, but I'm thinking about how quickly these numbers have gone up. Our US trend of new cases had a drop yesterday, but quickly rose again today, as well as the deaths. It is so frightening that this Coronavirus may be seasonal. I hope that with time, this may be eradicated. I wonder how this will affect how we Americans will be living.

Start of shift - April 9, 2020

I came in to work to find out that one of the patients I had been praying for had died. He was from a different country (not Italy) and just one year older than my husband. Who was he? Was he a father? A husband? A son? Maybe his mother still lived? Anyway, I was brokenhearted and realized, once again, that this life is temporary. I am sure the nurses and doctors who worked with him every day, and ministered to his needs, felt very much the same way. I didn't see it coming. I thought he had a better chance than some of the other patients. We lost two patients last night. The angel of death came and required two more souls…

I was asked to do a devotional for tomorrow morning on the bus ride back to our hotel. My heart is so quieted. I almost feel like I have no words. I was asking, "Lord, what do you want me to say?" We are in an occupation and place that faces the shadow of death daily. I found this simple verse, pieced in a long stretch of scripture that ministered to me. Probably taken out of context, but it doesn't matter in times like this. It just ministered to me and gave me comfort. Matthew 4:16 (KJV) says, "The people which sat in darkness saw great light; and to them which sat in the region and shadow of death light is sprung up."

Light. Your ever-present light. Your Holy Spirit. Your comfort.

Our God Who sees us and our circumstances knows us BY NAME. The same God knows the number of hairs on our heads and He takes note of every human who walks through the shadow of death!

Just past midnight April 9, 2020

Was pondering this day when I got up from sleeping, 7 hours after my night shift. I looked out the window of my hotel and saw little life passing by. By that hour (around 5PM), there were a few people with masks on and they were riding their bikes, some people with masks on and riding in their cars and on buses, and an ambulance that went by. I saw several men standing in front of a bank that was clearly closed, looking at their phones (of course, with masks on their faces). I saw a man with a mask on his face, walking his large, beautiful dog. Everything is closed. I saw a single movement in the town's square from a second-story building window. A resident was opening her window to tend to her flower boxes. I wonder where all the people are. They are quarantined in their homes. How are they faring? What strange times we are in. Honestly, it feels a little like I am in a strange movie.

Okay, things to remember if I have the opportunity to do another deployment. I have become a minimalist. And a minimalist brings only one small carry-on luggage and a small backpack. This time that was a mistake. (Insert "hard laugh" here). I wish dearly I had brought a warmer fleece coat. Yes, that would have been so nice. However, SP supplied me (along with many on my team, as we were not expecting the bitter cold and wind) a nice, much warmer coat, which I will leave for the next crew. It has certainly helped. Oh, and I do wish I had brought those wool socks I threw in my suitcase and decided to leave home! Don't skim on socks again, Natalie. Oh, hairpins. I have fly-away hair and hairpins under all this PPE would have been wonderful! And with my blessed, thick hair, what was I thinking by not bringing cream rinse?! By all means, bring TONS of lotion and toothpaste! I was going to be here for a month. What was I thinking?!

Our new patient, MY AGE, they are trying to save.

I don't want to give tonight's statistics on Italy, because they've gone up slightly. I'm making myself record this. I'm tired of even giving this a name… Near Rome, cases have gone up 26%. This terrible virus is wreaking havoc in pockets of places. The government had issued a mandatory quarantine, and yet I see much more traffic today. Cars, people. I guess people are just tired of being indoors all this time. I am sure I will get a taste of that in the states when I get home. "Lord, bring our team safely home. Be with the teams that are on the way. Be especially with the New York team."

US statistics 454K cases; 198K of which NY & NJ have. Florida is at 16K cases.

For someone like me, who doesn't work in emergency medicine, I walk into the ICU and see the nurses and docs trying to revive a man. He is my age. He had just been transferred over. The doctors and nurses are all working feverishly to try and save him. I go into the lab to do emergency blood gas and when I'm finished, I am suddenly itching all over. My calves inside my big bulky boots are itching. I'm thinking, "I'm allergic to this chlorinated water!" My scrubs, washed in such hot, bleached water, is causing my skin to react. My hair is thinning out! My scalp is itching! My neck hurts in this large and heavy face-shield! My shoulders hurt and I can't take Excedrin. The mask is causing me to breathe in too much CO2. My nose is rubbed raw! My face has dents from the masks. My nose is dripping and I can't touch my face. I am hot in this PPE. And I WANT to have a panic attack! Everything in my body is screaming, I WANT TO GO HOME! In my psyche, I am aware that I am also reacting to what I just saw. I want that patient to live! Live!!! Breathe!!!! Please God!

And strangely enough, almost immediately, I am speaking back to that voice and that panic. I AM FINE. I truly am. Life is going to be okay.

I have no doubts that it is the prayers of so many lifting up our team. I am okay. And I will be okay. And my rapid breathing slows down. I KNOW with all my heart that Christ has come and invaded my panic with peace. I am calm and I am okay. I will speak to that voice that I am doing this with God's help. We've got this.

…and the man they were trying to save, just passed. He was 57. My age. Lord, be with his family. This is a hard 24 hours.

I want to end this night shift by saying, that this has been in some ways the HARDEST deployment. I think, by that, I mean it has simply been the long hours and wearing of PPEs for so long. And death. And suffering. Even with that, it has also been the richest experience. I will never forget the talented, beautiful, and selfless people I have worked with, putting themselves in harm's way… sometimes scared and fearful, as they recommit their faith in our Lord, trusting Him with their very lives. To this point, NO ONE on our team has contracted COVID. Some have thought they might have it and have had a test to check, but no one has come up positive.

I have had the opportunity to listen to music in the lab. That has been such a gift! To hear worship music and even light-hearted music helps lift my spirits and remember that His eyes are on me and I am not alone. I. AM. NOT. ALONE.

If things get worse in our area of Florida, I hope I can get a crew to remember the medical workers in our town. Feeling such love from the people here has also been a huge gift!

I leave this night hoping that you can take time to listen to Michael W. Smith's Italian version of "Waymaker" by Sinach, as I have listened to this over and over, especially the Italian version! Franklin Graham and Michael Smith will be doing a service on Sunday in Central Park by the SP hospital.

Post deployment thoughts:

We are all affected when there is a loss. We are all sobered. Everyone keeps working, but there is a pervasive sadness. As the night wears on, as morning comes and the end of the shift is near – you can see the wear and tear of the night. We're not as light-hearted at "breakfast" as we eat almost motionlessly and make our way to bed soon after the sun rises. Still trusting God, but feeling the weight of the loss.

A Nurse's Perspective (Taylor Pitkin):

And this, friends, is the truth. This past month has not been defined by fear. It has been defined by gospel movement in a time where the one thing that is certain, is the hope we have in Jesus who died for our sins on the cross and was risen from the grave. Praise be to God!

11 LONELINESS

Evening of April 10, 2020

The days and nights are passing very quickly. I'm grateful for a busy night shift. The days are getting hotter here and the nights are still chilly, which I actually enjoy. We are preparing for the next Med Techs to come, which should be around 3 more days. I'm encouraged because I know that soon I will be on a plane to go home! I will miss the beautiful people here at camp and in Italy also. I wish my husband was here. I miss him more.

The people we have been in contact with have treated us so very well! I LOVE northern Italy and hope I can come back again someday. I think Italy in many ways has been my favorite country to visit (my second time here). I love the people, the language, the lyrical notes in their speech. And their love language is FOOD.

Well, it's a bit quiet this evening at the camp. Settling in for the next 11 hours, since I've been here for just one hour.

It appears in the US that things are SLOWING down! I pray with all my heart that trend continues. Official numbers are USA 489K cases, with NY & NJ having 225K of those. Florida is at 17K.

In Italy, we appear to be on a downward trend! The lowest numbers yet as far as cases which have had an outcome; deaths at 38%; discharged/recovered at 68%! When I came here the numbers were at 45% and 55%, respectively! Daily cases have gone up slightly, as well as deaths yesterday, but the curve is trending downwards!

Loneliness. It's a good subject to bring up. During a DART, you connect very closely with some and feel a bit detached from others. You cannot take anything personally. By that, I mean, we are all here for a job. Many (or most of us) are firstborns. We are all serious, focused, and some are not the outgoing type (and I would probably describe myself as an "Extrovert Introvert", who likes to interact but is sometimes shy) – and you can confuse that sometimes by thinking someone just doesn't like you. I don't believe that's the truth either! We are all different, from different backgrounds, sometimes different countries (we have US, Canadians, Brits and Italians here!) and THE common denominator in our lives is our faith in Jesus Christ. That is the glue that binds us all together.

In some of the prior missions I've been on, I'm so thankful that God gave me special friends that I connected with. I find that as I have gotten older, that I AM a people person. I love hearing stories of other's lives. I love hearing their journeys, and I love getting to know other people. On this DART, I have been so blessed to connect with some very special people, and I thank God He has lessened my loneliness. I haven't felt it too much, but I did especially tonight. I am reminded of several on the team tonight who have encouraged me, when they didn't even realize they had!

Post deployment thoughts: After the end of every shift, we doff (take off our PPE) methodically, and go to the changing tent to change into clean scrubs. We make our way to the bus station as the sun is rising and greet the day shift team. We cheer each other on! As our team gets on the bus, Casey has made sure someone is giving a 5-minute devotional. *It is water to our souls.*

April 11, 2020

Today must have been a bit warm, as getting to the tents was a little hot. As the night gets cooler, I enjoy it, as I do well in colder weather and it actually lessens my physical pain. Sure miss my family. As I get closer to leaving, I really am ready to see everyone, but I need to quarantine for 2 weeks. It's okay and I will consider it a blessing, because when have I had someone say, "You need to do NOTHING for two weeks?" I hope I can type up my journaling notes…and make soap and homemade bread. That is what's on the agenda! How exciting! I'm so happy I got to see my grandchildren before I came here. It was a blessing and that time will carry me for a little longer until I see them again. All my children are doing well, in spite of several losing jobs during this crisis.

It marvels me more and more as I meet such special people here… the cream of the crop. Today was Erin Cline's 30th birthday (night shift nurse). She is from Houston and works in Orthopedics. Asked today what she hoped she could do this next year and her answers were "to finish her pilot's license and finish reading through the Bible." To have such lofty goals… I am so enamored of these amazing young people.

Last night, I really enjoyed talking with Carolyn from Canada. She and her husband, Ian, came here together. They both served in the Arctic for a year, with another organization. They are both remarkable! Found out Carolyn sailed from age 9 to age 14 around the world with her parents and brother to 27 countries. (I have read countless accounts of sailors and we sailed with a friend to the Bahamas, so I was very interested!) I have to laugh because she said her parents are still adventure-seekers, hang-gliding into their 50s (um, I'm 57)! She has much more to her story, but many of these remarkable young people come from such adventurous and accomplished families! What a heritage!

Post deployment thoughts: I met so many wonderful, talented staff on this deployment. We each had 12-hour shifts. I tended to take a break twice in my shift before being done, so that meant coming in at 7PM break at 10:30PM another break at 2:30AM and then off at 7AM. Some of the nurses would work until 3AM until they took their 1st break! When you are wearing these PPEs, to have a break to take it off, offers the wearer a sense that they can keep going! Many times for the doctors and nurses, the needs of the patient came way before their need for a break.

12 QUIET THE PANIC

April 12, 2020

In Italy, cases which have had an outcome…the deaths have gone down another percentage point to 37%. Discharged/recovered up to 63%. The curve is definitely going down, but I see it rose very quickly and is taking longer to resolve itself. Cases themselves have gone UP again from 3,951 yesterday to 4,694 today. This may be a seasonal virus. I can't imagine. In so many ways, the world's way of life has dramatically changed.

Confirmed cases in the US are now at 528K. NY & NJ with 238K of that and with 10,810 deaths. Florida is at 18K cases. My eyes are on CO, TX, OK, MO, FL and Germany with my niece and her family there as well.

Our team is amazing. Everyone has the best attitude and CARE for our patients. It is a fun group and they enjoy anything to get a laugh or release of some of the stresses that go with this job. One of our patients in ICU was born with a condition that has its own challenges. He has the sweetest spirit. He is in his early 50s and on a ventilator. Everyone loves saying his name and encouraging him. He has the most beautiful spirit and they are doing everything they can to help save him. Every day, he is poked and prodded. He had to have a tracheotomy and that requires care. I am sure all these pokes are painful at times, but he manages a pleasant attitude most of the time anyway. "N" seems to be resting okay… but I have to say, to have the pleasant attitude he has had (and, of course, he will also be quick to express his unpleasantries)… and to maybe not fully understand why or where he is, is a gift from God. He is a blessing to us and everyone is fighting for him.

On another note, I have heard the ambulance much more again today. It seemed to get quiet this past week and now suddenly the sirens are going again. I don't know if people are getting out more, but I truly can't imagine. Our team is doing amazing. No one has gotten sick, thankfully. I pray with all my heart no one will get the virus. There is a 2-14 day incubation period, with 5 days being the average. I pray that with due diligence in taking vitamins and with God's plan and covering for my life, that I will not get it as well. I pray especially for our older team members, nurses and doctors, who are exposed much more on an hourly basis.

Evening of April 12, 2020

Wow, I am SUPER tired tonight! I'll be working the night shift, of course, but I'm about to drift off! I wonder if my body knows that I'll soon be headed home and I'm preparing for the long quarantine? I have all these plans of fun things to do when I get home… make soap, make homemade bread…maybe ride my bike if we're allowed, type up my journal notes. I never have a lack of things to do. This might be the first time in my life I've been told to do NOTHING. I am looking forward to it, but I do wish I could enjoy the beach!

Spoke with Dr. Paul Shumpert, and every year, he and his wife head a team to Nepal. I have always wanted to visit that beautiful country and I let him know that if they ever need some help… or a photographer, I would love to go and help! I have read so many books about Nepal and the Himalayas. I read about a Nepalese young woman who left the country… and about missionaries who spent their entire lives serving the country. It is a place I have imagined and to see it and the people in person would be amazing. He mentioned the altitude is around 12,000 feet and how easy it is to get altitude sickness if you are not acclimated. Rick & I would do well to visit Elijah (our son) for two weeks in Colorado, so I could get acclimated to the altitude in Nepal, if a trip was planned. After being gone for 30 days, a 12-day mission trip would seem like a breeze. Dr. Paul mentioned they would love a photographer and I could serve as a Pharmacist. (Insert smile.) I don't know if I could handle it, but it's now or never, as I'm getting older.

I wonder how I got this passion for travel and cultures? My Mom and Dad gave me a book when I was a young girl, titled "Tombi's Song" about a little African girl. Why did they choose that book? Mom also gave me a book of poetry by a Lebanese poet, Khalil Gibran. And, of course, I was given a Bible at some point in my life. When I was a little girl living in West Virginia, my parents attended a Nazarene Church. I distinctly remember going to Sunday School (before I could read) and my parents helping me memorize Psalms 23. What I didn't know as a child of 7, was that my Dad was battling lymphoma at age 29. What stresses my parents had to be under as a young family with 4 kids!! I am sure all these events in my life led me to where I am today. I had a grandfather who always encouraged me in my faith (in fact, my 3rd son is named after him). I'm so glad God has directed my life and keeps writing my story. I will say, though, that the most important thing I ever did was have my children… and raise them. I had such joy in doing that, though I wish I could go back and capture those times and not get weary. I wish I could have done an even better job being a parent. Do we all feel that way? I am super proud of each of my kids, and I have to remember that God will direct each of them, allowing them the right amount of pain, joys and victories, so that they might rely solely on Him in their lives.

The night is quiet. I am not able to run labs today because the hospital lab is closed (for Easter I believe). We had a short, fifteen-minute service this morning for Easter. Several songs ("Amazing Grace" by John Newton, sung in Italian) and Joey Garner spoke. Joey works as Staff Support in different countries and on different deployments. His wife also works in HR at Samaritan's Purse. I am very proud of the discernment with which SP works under, praying carefully before they hire someone. So, it may be quiet tonight. I'm encouraged. Some of the ICU patients seem to be "awakening". I pray their lab values look better and that they will come out of this. There is one young guy, age 57 like me, and I saw him "awaken" from his deep slumber and from being on a ventilator. I pray he improves more and more.

Every so often, I feel a tinge of panic. Will I somehow get this virus on me? Will I get sick? I put all of these things out of my mind very quickly. Only GOD has my life. He determines my steps and my life. I have done my due diligence wearing the PPEs, being cautious…trusting Jesus and trusting the "science". But ultimately,

God determines my life. I pray often that our entire team will leave here well and NO ONE on this team will get COVID-19.

Italy reports 431 deaths, the lowest since March 19th.

USA has 551K cases. NY & NJ having 250K of those with 11,700 deaths. Florida is at 19,347 cases.

I love you all. Be home before you and I know it! Can't wait! Everyone be well!

A Nurse's Perspective (Taylor Pitkin):

One final thought I want to share:

"Because you have made the Lord your dwelling place – the Most High, who is my refuge - no evil shall be allowed to befall you, no plague come near your tent." Psalms 91:9-10 (ESV)

A Doctor's Perspective (Dr. Mark Agness):

"Do not forget to show hospitality to strangers, for by so doing some people have shown hospitality to angels without knowing it." Hebrews 13:2 (NIV)

"N" was no angel. At least he didn't act like one during most of my brief time with him. He would resist our attempts to turn him, grab the railing and refuse to let go, wave us off with a finger indicating his displeasure. He would turn and ignore us in what, I presume, was an attempt to dismiss us and make us disappear. He was intermittently feisty and ornery. Kind and loving demeanors could turn on a dime and become incredibly challenging and contrary.

Yet, on better days, when we weren't constantly doing tasks he found uncomfortable or unpleasant, he would smile and blow kisses to the nurses, allow us to hold his hand and soothe him. He loved to have his head rubbed and allowed the nurses to "gel" his hair each morning with water into whatever configuration seemed to suit the mood of the day. Later in my tenure, we were able to get him up to a recliner and even take him outside to experience the sun (at least the day shifters did). This was no small feat given his weakness and reluctance to be moved. An "N report" was a staple of each shift change wherein the departing nurse (and doctor) would recount the day's successes and challenges as they related to this particular patient.

He was unique amongst our ICU patients. In his early fifties, he was our youngest patient. He, like others, arrived intubated and deeply sedated. He was one of the first patients received by the RCU and was there at my departure nearly five weeks later. Moreover, "N" has a disability. His ability to communicate was never clear. As he awakened, the translators attempted to communicate with him in Italian. It was never obvious that he processed their speech or requests. He never seemed to follow the simple commands. "Squeeze my hand." "Close your eyes." All seemed lost on him. Or perhaps he ignored them as he frequently chose to do with us.

His hospital course had significant ups and downs. At one point extubated, only to be reintubated when his ability to exhale carbon dioxide was found to be inadequate. Infections, aspiration of stomach contents into the lungs, ventilator setbacks were all part of his course. We developed a numbering system to keep track of our patients. Days in the hospital/ Days on the ventilator/ Days in our RCU. "Mr. Z 20/10/7". On my departure, "N" had been in the hospital roughly 40 days, the majority of it at the SP RCU.

It was hard for me to pass "N's" bed without stopping to tell him hello, hold his hand, or stroke his head. Sometimes he received this gratefully, sometimes passively allowing the gestures, and at others withdrawing or giving the imperious finger wave that suggested he had had enough of me and that he wished me gone. At times he seemed distant and at others engaged. Working the night shift, "N" was awake a lot. We did everything we could think of to allow him to sleep. Lights off, minimal stimulation, setting the ventilator to help him avoid the coughing that plagued him later in his stay. He didn't sleep much.

It was also hard not to feel empathy and angst for "N". Our other patients were, at least at times, cognitively aware and could process their situation with the help of the interpreters. I didn't have that level of comfort with "N". Did he know where he was? Did he know who these masked people were? Did he understand where his caretakers were and why they weren't visiting him? Did he have any idea why we did so many things that seemed uncomfortable or unpleasant? Was he afraid? Angry? Depressed? I really couldn't answer any of those questions. It bothered me and all who cared for "N". More than that, I think it galvanized us all to do all in our power to get him out of the ICU and to a setting where he could be with his family and recover basking in their care and love.

I came to love "N" as did others. I couldn't help it nor did I try to rationalize it. He is a unique individual in a terribly challenging situation under frightening circumstances. I thought of him frequently, prayed for him often, and made every attempt I could think of to make his stay in the surreal surroundings of the ICU tolerable. On my return to the United States I requested updates on his condition and dreamed of reunions with his caretakers. Whether "N" ever comes to understand the trajectory of events over the past weeks or not seemed immaterial. Whether he ever came to understand who we were or in any way comprehend our love for him wasn't important. I don't think any of us desired any sort of reciprocation. We just learned to love him for who he was and wanted him better.

As is often the case when we give of ourselves, we receive more in return. This was certainly the case here. The occasional smile, hand squeeze, and gradual improvement were reward enough. The fact that he proved to me my passion for the less fortunate and empathy for those in crisis wasn't jaded, was a huge joy and reassurance. It drew me a little closer to God who, in spite of our disdain for His blessings, continues to love us. Not unlike "N", I find myself not understanding the circumstances of my situation. I become fearful, or angry. I play silly passive aggressive games to get my will. In those times, God soothes me, patiently awaiting that small gesture that suggests I understand, if only a little.

Did we host an angel? Probably not, but I'm happy to believe that if we did, we did our best to do so in a way that would bring a smile to God's lips...or "N's".

13 HEADED TO HOME SWEET HOME!

April 14, 2020

Today is April 14th and I can't believe it, but I'm headed HOME! Home is such a beautiful word and I'm so grateful to be headed there! God has sustained me on this trip! I am NOT a strong person! In fact, sometimes I feel very frail but it has only been His strength! I'm so grateful!

Yesterday morning, just before my night shift was over, I found out I was leaving that night/morning at 2:15AM, TO GO HOME. I found out it was my last shift. I don't know why my dear coworker was leaving a day after me (maybe it is because she is fulltime staff, directing the laboratory at SP), but I pray her rest comes soon. She arrived before me and is older than me, so I pray she indeed goes home on the 15th! Lord, let it be!

The New York team needs our prayers desperately! Strong winds and rains have pummeled them! My heart is broken for them, as I know they are suffering. I pray they will be okay! We had winds (30 mph gusts) and that was strong! Several shelves toppled in the ICU tents, so that had to be a bit frightening!

My friend, Dr. Peter Kwan, asked for prayers for the New York team, of which he is serving. The winds and rain are hard on the staff and the patients are scared in the tents. "Lord, still the wind and dry things out for them! Give them wellness and strength!"

I will finish out my deployment by arriving home and will quarantine for two weeks. During that time, more teams will come to replace those of us who are leaving. "Lord, continue to be the strength of those who are serving, and for the patients who need Your touch!"

Post deployment thoughts:

How quickly a new day and answered prayer came! The next morning, after the storm in New York, a photo was taken near the SP camp. The winds and storm had ceased and a gorgeous rainbow covered the area…

April 15, 2020

Thank you, God. I MADE IT HOME past midnight on April 15th! Home Sweet Home. Everything seems fresh and new when you have been gone for nearly a month. I finish out my 14-day quarantine on April 29, 2020. A new job will hopefully ensue soon.

Today, April 28, 2020, the CURVE for Italy is finally taking a sure downturn. There are still 105K active cases, with only 2% of those serious or critical. Closed cases are 72% discharged/recovered and down to 28% deaths (at 27,359).

Post-Deployment Thoughts (Natalie Evans):

Have you ever been in the middle of something that seemed very hard at the time, but looking back, you were so glad you did it AND you were also so glad it was over! That was Italy's Coronavirus pandemic for me! Maybe it was an age-thing. Maybe I'm just not as strong (or never was strong) as I used to be – but nonetheless, this deployment was hard for me. I look back on the experience, I am filled with gratitude that I was able to assist in some way. I am grateful for the beautiful friendships and amazing people I met. At the time, I prayed, "Lord, I cannot do this without You!" And that was completely true! I *knew* HE was my strength! He was the *only* reason I could continue and the only reason I could finish! I came home and finished my 14-day quarantine. I had one full 24-hour time of extreme body-aches and nausea, to the extreme. I wondered if I had some different type of symptoms related to COVID not yet known! All of us continued to check our temperatures morning and night. Things at home were just like in Italy. Restaurants were closed. The streets were empty. After my quarantine, people still wore masks. I wondered how the average person was faring, since I had been gone for nearly 30 days. April 12th, I recorded 19K cases of COVID-19 in Florida. On May 3rd, Florida opened up restaurants to 25% capacity. By May 16th, Florida has seen 44K cases. (At time of printing June 6th, Florida has seen 60,183 cases). To date, no one really knows how this will continue. This is still a mystery to our country and to our leaders. And to date, what I do know is that God has every part of my life.

A Nurse's Perspective (Shannon Wood):

There's no place in the world that people need help the most than in a disaster situation and specifically in the ICU. To be able to serve in a way that helps people when they are at their darkest time, when they are at their most desperate, and when I can offer them not only the skills to help them physically, but to encourage them mentally, physically and spiritually, that is my passion. That is what I am on this earth to do, at least for this season in my life. And to be able to see that to fruition, there's no place in the world I'd rather be than right here in the ICU in the field. There is no place I'd rather be than right here in Italy, working in the ICU during a pandemic, where the pandemic is the worst. It's an honor to be able to be part of this, to have God put such a desire in my heart that He has slowly, step by step fulfilled that. My story is not over and I'm not sure what the future holds or where He'll take me next and what He'll do with me, but I know it's the most exciting adventure I've been on and I never want it to stop. When I go home, I will probably think a lot more about this, but the thing I keep reflecting on about this DART as I'm leaving, is how much I loved these patients. That is something I can't take credit for personally. That is not me loving them; that is Jesus loving them through me. It's addicting to share about that with people. It's addicting to share the love of Christ to people and to be used in that way. I loved my patients as well as I could with the grace that God gave me.

14 NYC- NOT SINCE THE CIVIL WAR

A Doctor's Perspective (Dr. Peter Kwan):

Let me introduce myself. My name is Peter Kwan, and I am a recently retired Family Medicine Physician and had been an ER doc, in private practice, large group practice, and faculty of a FM residency program in the various stages of my career. I have a BA in Biology from University of Texas (UT) in Austin and completed my medical degree from the University of Texas Medical School in the Houston Medical Center. My residency in family medicine was also a UT program. I have been associated with Samaritan's Purse (SP), a Christian faith-based international relief and disaster response group, for the past 13 years at the time of this writing. I have served as a member of the World Medical Missions branch (WMM) and the Disaster Assistance Response Team (DART) during this time. The purposes of these two branches of SP are distinct and you may find out more on SP's website. My incredible wife, Shirley, served with me on numerous medical missions with our home church and with SP's Operation Heal Our Patriots program in Alaska for the past seven years. We have two children; Christopher, the elder, is a high school chemistry teacher, and Melissa, is a Pediatric ER physician and hospitalist. Both Christopher and Melissa have been in short term missionary service as well.

I have been asked by others, and I also asked myself: why serve? My answers are that God has given each of us a talent. There is something; a skill, special knowledge, either innate or learned that sets us apart from each other. Whatever that talent is may earn you a living in your lifetime but also provides an ability to help others. Almost all physicians earn a comfortable living or better in terms of monetary rewards, and it would be easy to sit back and enjoy such rewards. I believe there is a higher calling that one may hear in one's heart and respond to when the needs arises. This often requires a leap of faith to answer this call and step out of the comfort zone into the unknown.

When I joined SP's DART, I was told in the orientation process that disasters would occur in the world every year. SP is ready to respond to the worst ones when invited. We have the resources, material, and well-trained personnel to do so rapidly. Speed is the key to saving and restoring lives. This is my 7th DART or similar deployment with SP and each experience is so vastly different. The countries and cultures were different, the challenges and our work were different each time. One thing stays the same: we are to be the "hands and feet" of Jesus Christ our Savior to give our time, skills and love to a hurting people.

In March of 2020, SP had put out e-mails seeking DART availability for a COVID-19 response in Italy. Within a week, a team and the Emergency Field Hospital (EFH) was on the ground in Italy. In just 2 to 3 short days, the hospital was up and accepting patients. Immediately after, there was a call for a second team to be assembled for a COVID-19 response in New York City, where the health care system was stretched thin due to the sudden rise in the number of infected patients. Never had the SP DART been deployed inside the USA. The EFH, when deployed in the past, often represented the highest level of skills, technology and personnel available in that entire region. Now we would be in Central Park of NYC. The last time there was an emergency field hospital in Central Park was during the Civil War. This was an historic event.

I had deployed in the past to an African missionary hospital, then to an Iraqi war zone where live-fire went on day and night, and to several infectious disease treatment centers. I had gone without any fear of personal safety and, with God's protection, had returned safely. This call was different. The enemy was new - an infection which had no pharmacologic treatment, no immunization and was highly infectious. My personal medical conditions and age group put me at high risk for morbidity and mortality if I were to be infected with this SARSCoV-2 virus. I wanted to respond to this call for service, but I had so much anxiety that I had never felt before. I knew I had to answer the call, but the anxiety level was extremely high as I stepped on the plane, my point of no return. Only prayers gave me peace, but fear and anxiety always returned.

The first three days after my arrival in NYC, the EFH was being assembled and supplies distributed. I did what I could to help that process but I felt more at a loss, because the medical part of the response had not yet started. As parts of the EFH took shape, it became more like home, looking like the other EFHs in the past. My fear subsided with prayer as I donned my PPE (Personal Protective Equipment) for the first time into the hot zone to receive our first patient. I was in my element again and all fears and anxiety resolved, for God had put me here to represent Him. When I crossed that imaginary line between Hot and Green, my resolve was committed and ready to do what I had been trained to do. I was to provide the medical care as part of an incredibly assembled team of God's army in this fight. Each piece of the PPE was (per Kelly Sites, RN) like us putting on the "Armor of God" to do battle. On a morning devotion, our chaplain said God breathed life into man, but this disease was here to rob the breath out of each of our patients. Although our physical therapeutics were limited, our spiritual presence of love, compassion, and fellowship were our most powerful defenses and offenses.

Our EFH is a small community. The majority of the staff are medically trained providers; physicians, nurses, CRNAs, EMTs, pharmacists, Xray and laboratory technologists, but there is a large support staff of medical administrators, Chaplains, IT, biomed specialists, electricians, plumbers, carpenters, people who fix things that we break, cleaners, security, logistics, communication specialists, photojournalists, writers and the list goes on. We all work together to achieve the goal of care and ministry to our patients. The hours are long. There are no days off. We work every day, our teams are lean, and no one may be spared - but we all knew that going in. No one ever complains about our tasks.

We started slowly with just a few patients that first day as a warm-up.

By the 2nd day the hospital was nearly half full and the third day we were nearing full capacity. There was a sharp learning curve on how to take care of our patients. All our patients were transfers from several Mount Sinai Hospitals that were stressed to their limits. All had either tested positive or had clinical findings of COVID-19. Some patients were recovering, already improving, and others were just diagnosed. Many were very sick. This illness was capable of causing a sudden downward change in our patients without warning. The patient could be sitting up eating breakfast, and then intubated on a ventilator in our ICU before lunch time. Some struggled for several days on oxygen before slow improvement began and declined a little each day. There were predictable trends that helped us to anticipate the needs and level of care, but we had to be so vigilant.

We had some deaths, but we had a far greater number of recovered discharges. Our staff prayed with the patients (with their permission naturally), and if they desired, our chaplain could come in for visits. We had many become believers during their stay. When our patients were discharged, they would ring a cowbell to signify to the rest of the hospital - we have a win in God's column. The staff that were available would come out of the wards to clap and cheer the patient as they walked out of the hospital to their waiting families.

New York City, has a large and diverse population with individuals and special interest groups that clearly were opposed to the idea that a Christian group had established a foothold in their backyard. They had protested us, but that was short-lived and almost unnoticed. Others would spend days videoing from some high grounds and posting on social media unsupported conspiracy theories. There are others who denied COVID-19 even existed or saw no reason for any infection control measures, because it interfered with their personal freedoms. I do understand that the United States was founded on freedoms, but we must consider the effect of consequences to other family members and neighbors. No matter what the statistics, many died and many more would die prematurely from this disease. My feelings during this time of uncertainty is if you do not believe COVID-19 is real and that it will not affect you, I pray that it will not touch your lives; but please do what you can to help with the containment. Freedom is of little value without responsibility.

I thank all the New Yorkers who came out to help assemble this EFH. So many came along SP with their gifts of time, physical labor, financial assistance, and encouragement. Many businesses and family members of patients provided us with incredible meals (a rare luxury on DART deployments). Your cards and gifts of flowers reminded us of your support. So heartwarming to hear each day at 7PM during hospital staff shift-change - the horns, sirens, bells, clanging of pots and pans, clapping and noisemaking that let us know the City was behind us, cheering us in our work.

In closing, I ask continued prayers for our SP family all over the world. They have important and difficult tasks to face. I ask for prayers for our team members on the front line, for protection against this disease, for strength and stamina in their difficult work. Pray for our patients' complete and rapid recovery and that they will come to know Jesus Christ as their Savior, as they come through this life changing event.

Peter Kwan, M.D.

Samaritan's Purse

WMM and DART volunteer.

A Nurse's Perspective: (Katie Kunnen)

Katie Kunnen DNP, NP-C, APRN
Katherine (Katie) Kunnen is an assistant professor at Calvin University. She is an undergraduate alumnus of Calvin and received her DNP from the University of Michigan-Flint. She recently celebrated her two-year anniversary with her husband Luke, who works as a private music teacher. The deployment to NYC was Katie's third response with Samaritan's Purse medical Disaster Assistance Response Team. She previously deployed to Iraq and Ecuador. During the summer, she works for Signify Health providing home health visits for Medicare/Medicaid patients, while also working on research related to nursing simulation, and diversity and inclusion.

When I first attempted to reflect on my time in NYC, it was all a great blur. I had to go back and look at my WhatsApp messages to piece together the days. This is largely because I got very little sleep the first week and a half. I think I averaged 5-6 hours of sleep per night, and my time sheet says I worked 14-16 hours most days that first week. In that case, it truly is a miracle that I didn't catch the common cold, let alone the coronavirus. I normally catch a cold as soon as I am deprived of less than 7 hours of sleep per night. Of course, there was never any question of me catching the coronavirus. We were so well protected by Samaritan Purse's rigorous infectious protocols and PPE similar to Ebola gear. In some ways, I felt very guilty that we were so well protected when all around the world there were nurses working with PPE shortages. However, I had to remember that self-care is essential to caring for others and it would do no one good if I ended up on a ventilator myself. However, I NEVER took for granted the privilege of the protection SP provided us.

Ever since my first DART in Ecuador, I have always prepared myself for DARTs knowing that the devil throws all sorts of sly temptations and challenges in these situations. My friends and family know that I often refer to dragons and nits. Before I knew I was going to NYC, I wrote this in an email to friends and family:

"Psychologically, a dragon - though it shakes us to the core - fuels the fight in us. The average human is excited to rise to a new challenge - just look at the headlines about people sewing masks, restaurants donating food for children without school meals, and children writing to the nursing homes, etc. It is easy to rush to the front lines and be heroic.

It is much harder to respond with grace to the child who is whining for the umpteenth time for an unreasonable desire, or to try to live in close quarters with someone when all their habits seem be driving you up the wall, or to do your work remotely and quietly without getting any praise for doing so, or to do the dishes which have piled up and you are sure you are the ONLY one doing them - without becoming passive aggressive, or so on and so forth."

The "nits" encountered on a DART can include anything from jealousy over who gets put on day shift versus night shift – not only because nights shifts are hard on your body, but also because you don't get to see successful discharges on nights, or feeling unseen when some of your teammates are getting media coverage and there's not one single picture proving you were there. It can be a blow to your pride when you are an ER doc or an NP, but you get put on ward duty or demoted to a nursing position etc. So, I always say the key to every DART is to be completely humble and willing to serve in whatever way is given to you. Serving on a DART requires a certain kind of obedience that Jesus modelled best. I don't think I've ever been as well prepared for a DART as for this one, because my church was going through 40 days of Lent series on centering prayer.

I think one of the greatest errors a Christian can make – is to neglect time spent sitting at the Lord's feet. In the Catholic tradition, there is a rich history of a practice called "recollection". Recollection, for those of us unfamiliar with the Catholic concept, "as understood in respect to the spiritual life, means attention to the presence of God in the soul… It is the same as interior solitude in which the soul is alone with God." (Devine, 1911). Spiritual disciplines such as centering prayer, solitude, and silence help us practice this attention to the presence of God. In a world and culture that values productivity and achievement, this can be almost impossible to accept. Yet one advent, Loretta Ross-Gotta challenged me with this insight: "What is it that delivers Christ into the world - preaching, art, writing, scholarship, social justice? Those are all gifts well worth sharing. But preachers lose their charisma, scholarship grows pedantic, social justice alone cannot save us. In the end, when all other human gifts have met their inevitable limitation, it is the recollected one, the bold virgin with a heart in love with God who makes a sanctuary of her life, who delivers Christ who then delivers us." (2001, p. 97). As an enneagram type 2, natural "Martha", it is absolutely critical that I am reminded by Jesus that Mary chose that which would not be taken from her – His own precious presence – and by remembering His presence and work, I can then rest from my own work by remembering He is the true Savior of the world – not me!

Nursing has always been a challenge for me, because the stress of meeting the patient's needs (while also keeping them safe with all the tasks that need to get done) often leaves me unfocused, impatient, and frustrated. I find myself going so fast that I whip the gait belt around and knock my poor patient on the knee with the hard end of the belt – or in the case of New York, I accidently shove someone's oxygen mask up their face and hit their nose funny, because it is change of shift and they have diarrhea and need to get to the commode NOW, but I'm also trying-to give change of shift report to the night nurses, so that I can make the shuttle before it leaves and I have to wait another 15 minutes. Satan always gets you with the lie that there's "not enough" or you're going to "miss out". In the end, what if you have to wait another 15 minutes? It's good to slow down and wait! Anyway,

I gave that example to make it clear that I still totally failed on some accounts. There are no perfect people. BUT for the first time I can ever recall, there were multiple moments over multiple days where I recognized that I was becoming anxious or stressed, and leaned into the moment to slow down, let go of the need for control, and surrendered everything back to Jesus.

Our book for Lent had us practice spending 20 minutes of silence before God's presence, but it would bring your wandering mind back to God's presence. Mine was "consent" or "surrender". So, when I was out in the field, rushing to empty the commode for what seemed like the 20th time, I would sometimes gaze at a certain tree and speak my word of "consent" and return to my patients a much more peaceful, grace-filled person. It probably didn't always seem like it to my peers, because I still zoomed around quite a bit (my nickname was the energizer bunny) and got frustrated. "I WROTE THE ORDERS AND SENT THEM 3 FREAKING DAYS AGO" (direct quote when I was missing patient's home maintenance medications). However, like I said, there were many days where I succeeded in letting go of the anxiety and taking extra time for things like putting the pulse oximeter on my extra anxious patient every time she requested, or getting hot water and coffee for all the patients in the ward because they absolutely adored hot beverages. (Let me tell you, that process was not easy until we got a Kerig in the "hot zone". It involved radioing over the walkie talkie and hoping someone heard me, or typing a painful text message on my phone with two pairs of gloves through a plastic baggie and hoping someone would see the message and create 6-10 cups of hot water/coffee and remember to include the tea bags and find some way to cart them over to the donning zone AND that I would get the return text notifying me they were ready BEFORE they were already stone cold).

There wasn't a typical day for me in the beginning, because I was roped into administrative duties and did everything from building cots, creating admission and discharge orders for the providers, teaching

PPE sessions, tracking everyone down for credentialing, and problem solving the most random things such as... the doctors need their phones in the "hot zone", but they couldn't dunk them in chlorine coming out, so can we get some Ziploc bags to cover them - ok now I'll go run to supply and ask Heidi if we can get some ordered because we have none – and can we get something else for the long term – like fanny packs? We ended up with Home Depot aprons. They were da bomb! Even once I started going into the "hot zone" and helping with patient care, I was still at the EFH working until 10-11PM most nights that first week or so (hence the lack of sleep).

After the first week, the average day for me looked like waking up at 5:40AM, taking my temperature, getting ready to go quickly, putting on a mask and leaving the hotel at 6:00AM. I would usually take the 15 minutes it took to get to site to read my passage from my Lent book and take a few moments of centering prayer – unless I had woken up earlier on my own and been able to take that time first thing. Occasionally, I would share a passage to the group chat. Some examples of passages I shared are below:

The pace of modern living (especially in a field hospital) causes us to lose consciousness of God in the moment, even when God is present. We need prayer and scripture to remind us that we would be unable to do anything without God's gifts to us. (paraphrased from Muyskens, 2006, p. 104).

How to incorporate prayer as self-care (and a reminder to surrender in obedience to God in the midst of adversity or tension): "In the daily round, I became aware of tension or pain in my body that manifests a feeling, body sensation, emotion or thought. At that point, I let myself sink into the sensation. Then I used the word 'welcome' as a prayer word and embraced the pain or tension. I welcome God's presence and activity in it. I let go of my desire for security and approval. I give up control and release my desire to change the situation. I surrender to the love of God and the healing action of Christ." (Muyskens, 2006, p. 110).

"When I became anxious to get the job done and acted hastily, the effort did not go well. When I decided to apply my understandings from contemplative prayer, I entered the work with more attention to what I was doing. Instead of anxiously awaiting the end of the task, I entered into the joy of doing it and doing it as well as I could... A contemplative attitude makes tedious work more enjoyable. Every task becomes an opportunity to share in the activity of God… (Muyskens, 2006, p. 115).

You can see how those reflections resonated with what I was saying before – about feeling anxious and acting hastily – or becoming aware of the sensation of tension/pain and welcoming God into it while letting go of control or the desire to change the situation!

Then we would arrive on site, I would stuff my face with the delicious croissant breakfast sandwiches we got and debate whether I would drink coffee or water that day or dehydrate myself on purpose, so I wouldn't have to leave the ward until later in the day. Since we had to doff our PPE completely when leaving the hot zone, we mostly tried to leave only a few times in the day. Some of us only managed to leave once during the 12 hours for our lunch break. During breakfast, we would hear devotions from one of our leadership staff or the chaplains. It was always an encouraging time – though sometimes we were half asleep and frozen. Then I would rush to use the bathroom and then don all my PPE so that the night shift could get out on time. Debra, my partner in crime, aka the other nurse in the ward, and I would receive a shift report and start in immediately on vitals. Our ward held up to 14 patients, so we would typically divide up the caseload between us. Usually we didn't have more than 6 patients, but it was still busy getting vitals done (the old-fashioned way – with a BP cuff and stethoscope, slow oral thermometers, and counting respirations for a full minute), medications, and breakfast/hot tea and coffee distributed. Because our patients were so sick, sometimes even getting breakfast out was too exhausting for them. So, every meal Debra and I would spend time taking everything out of the bag, opening juice lids, cutting up main courses etc. Then as you already know, in the morning I would go through the ordeal of getting everyone a hot drink of some type. It was made more difficult when there were certain patients who wanted ONLY sweet and low… Hahaha. There's always that one particular patient! One day, I was acting hastily and spilled hot water on myself giving myself a 1st degree burn… So quickly I forgot my own advice! I think this is why Jesus told us to "REMEMBER" during communion.

If we were lucky and got done with the morning rush around 10-10:30AM we would start walking the patients. Walking was important to keep up their physical strength – but it was also our test for discharge. If someone could walk on room air two lengths of the tent without desaturating below 90% and without becoming tachycardic, they could discharge. Then our ward provider could write them discharge notes and the charge ward nurse could work on discharge transport with them. Due to NP Karmen's brilliant idea, we also acquired cow bells which we would have the patients ring furiously as they were discharging – and that would signal for everyone to come out of the wards and cheer them. It was one of the most encouraging and delightful quirks to this particular DART.

Then it would be time for the patient's lunches. After making sure blood glucose checks were done, distributing lunches, and administering insulin, one of us would run out to eat our own lunch– often leaving behind the other all alone to man the tent. There was a float RN who was supposed to check in, but they were floating for all five wards, so if we didn't need them, we tried not to hog them. As the afternoon progressed, we would discharge patients and start receiving admissions. It was usually pretty manageable unless we got slammed with 3+ admissions within an hour – which only happened a few times. One of the more challenging aspects of our ward was that it was "mixed" and had male and female patients, so therefore we had to get patients to the bathroom in the privatized corner if at all possible. Yet some of our patients were desaturating incredibly. I remember taking a patient to the bathroom on 8L of O2 with a facemask and checking his O2 sat once he got back to bed and finding it at 53%. I was like – we CANNOT repeat this! Patients with this low of oxygen need to use a bedside commode or bedpan!!!! So, then we would rig up sheets on either side of the patient and hold them to give them privacy on the commode. This was all well and good provided we didn't have more than two patients that needed this kind of help, because what happens when four patients all need to go to the bathroom and need assistance? So, I guess it's a lot like regular nursing, except you have a 6-7 patient load without having a nurse tech to help with vitals or ambulation. I know that it doesn't seem like a "big deal" if you can't get a patient to the bathroom right away, but if you're the patient and you have an accident, it IS a huge deal to your dignity!

Anyway, if the day was calm enough, we might sneak off for a second 15-minute break. With doffing and donning, this really just means running straight to the bathroom, jugging a water bottle, and coming straight back in – but even that was a relief! Often, I would keep an eye on the Whatsapp chats and if it looked like someone was having a hard time, or missing a medication, I would try to assist with their needs. Toward the end of shift, I would write a small nursing progress note – especially if the patient had made progress or lost ground. If I had time, I would sort through the night medications due and clip them to the MAR board, so the night RN's would have everything set. Finally, we would write up a report sheet for the night nurses and put a bible verse at the top to encourage them. After the shift report, it was a mad dash to doff, use the bathroom, shed our dirty scrubs, grab a dinner, and head immediately to the shuttle to get back to the hotel. We couldn't eat in the shuttles – and I always showered first thing at the hotel, so I usually didn't eat until 8 or 8:30PM at night. Strangely with all the back-end loading and carbohydrates, I still did not gain my COVID-19lbs… 😊

Life was still a little atypical even as I began to get into a rhythm, because I had responsibilities at home. Though I had finished my faith community nurse continuing education class, there were still questions from RNs about how to apply what they learned in the now COVID-19 situation. It was a crash course into public health for many of them. Prior to COVID-19, I had started a standardized patient program and we managed to get a few sessions in before we had to shut down, so I needed to finalize the payroll process and make sure they got paid. While I was gone my department interviewed and hired a new faculty. Students still had questions about assignments. My research assistant went back to Korea, so I needed to make sure her position ended correctly. So, every night while eating dinner at 8:30PM, I would browse through emails and try to meet the priority needs.

Once I made it home, I was thankful for the interaction with my advisees over video conference and hours of catch up grading, since many of my peers struggled with the isolation of quarantine. However, now that the grading is finally wrapping up, I am relieved to have some time to process the event. The New York deployment was unique for many reasons - setting up in Central Park of all places, having the barrier of the "hot zone" versus "green zone", watching the complex media reaction, combating the severity of patient illness. Everyone always asks about the impact of the DARTs and I can't help but wonder if there's something wrong with me when I say there is no huge impact. I don't experience trauma or PTSD. I don't feel out of place or restless now that I'm back in the daily groove of my life. I don't believe that God worked through me more powerfully. Perhaps it's because I have a deep-seated belief that God doesn't often work in great pillars of fire, but prefers quiet whispers. Also, there's that famous quote which is probably incorrectly ascribed to Mother Teresa about us not all being able to do great acts, but certainly able to do small acts with great love. I think that is the call for the rest of us who aren't on the front lines. Overall, the impact of this DART is very similar to others. It reveals to me the power of the "nits" and how easily I am pulled into comparison games. How exhaustion brings out pettiness and irritation. How quick I am to judge and to complain. How easily I want to claim the hero role as my own. But hopefully, as I have revealed, I am no hero - just an ordinary human trying to be obedient to God. I set Jesus before me as the author and perfecter of my faith. His human life was quiet and ordinary until God called him to fulfill his destiny - and even then, that destiny did not result in the powerful overthrow of corrupt authorities, but in the submission to a humiliating and painful death. My desire is to do the same and be obedient unto death. Soli deo gloria.

A Doctor's Perspective (Dr. Michael Post):

My name is Michael Post, MD. I grew up in Grand Rapids, Michigan and attended Calvin University, then Wayne State University School of Medicine, graduating in 1980. I have practiced internal medicine in Fremont, Michigan; Marinette, Wisconsin and finally geriatrics in Grand Rapids, Michigan, retiring in December, 2017. I have four children and seven grandchildren with two more on the way. I have been glued to the love of my life, Barb, since we met at age 15 - we have been together for 50 years, married for 44 years!

I was introduced to medical missions by a good friend who has since died, Dr. Lorrence Hnatuk. I have served for Samaritan's Purse WMM on the Ruth Bell River Boat in 2013 and 2015. I worked with SP DART this spring for my first time. When I first heard that SP was setting up a field hospital in NYC to help with the COVID-19 pandemic, I knew that I had to go. After discussing it with Barb and praying for guidance, I told her "I can't not go." I knew that I would regret what I felt to be a calling if I stayed home.

I came to NYC on March 30, 2020 with two other SP DART workers, Katy and Christina. We were the only ones in the plane.

The SP DART team had been setting up for two days and it took them only two more days to begin taking in patients. It was a phenomenal undertaking by the staff, putting up a 68-bed ward and 10-bed ICU hospital in working order in four days, helped tremendously by their experience in Iraq, Italy, and all over the world. The first wave medical team helped set up the tents with the staff.

A typical day began at 4:30AM with a shower, devotions and a call to my wife. We were then transported to the field hospital site in Central Park at 6AM, changed into scrubs, grabbed breakfast, had staff devotions and announcements. At 7AM, a medical provider staff meeting updated us on patient conditions. Then, the process of entering the "hot zone" in PPE took place where we rounded on the patients, updated labs, examined X-rays, had bedside ultrasounds with Mount Sinai staff, adjusted oxygen and medications. New patients came in, many from Mount Sinai Queens Hospital, and were admitted to our men's and women's ward tents. Many would be treated with medication and supplemental oxygen and be discharged home, but some progressed to higher and higher oxygen requirements with nonrebreathers and CPAP until the only way to deliver enough oxygen to keep them alive was by mechanical ventilation, which was done in the ICU tent. I was not fully prepared for what I saw - not only raging pulmonary disease caused by the virus and their immune systems fighting it, but multi-systemic disease. COVID-19 attacks the lungs, the coagulation cascade, the oxygen transport system, the heart, the kidney, the liver, GI system, and neurologic system. These were truly the sickest patients I have seen - tachycardic, tachypneic, hyperdynamic on Echo, diaphoretic, over-breathing and fighting the ventilator if not sedated and paralyzed. At times, their secretions would set up and obstruct their endotracheal tubes, refractory to lavage and suction, requiring replacement. Many came in terrified; they were literally being asphyxiated. This difficult path for them leading to invasive ventilation was made worse by their isolation from their families. We were their only human contact. We tried to allow some access to their families by messaging, frequent calls and updates, and FaceTime with phones. Many of the sickest would progress to needing more services than we could provide in the tents, such as dialysis and extracorporeal membrane oxygenation or ECMO.

The Mount Sinai Hospital Critical Care Medical staff was always so ready and helpful. If we had a patient with suspected pulmonary embolus, they would drop everything and immediately don PPE and help us examine them with bedside ultrasound. They would quickly take patients to their own ICU across the street whenever their expertise and diagnostics could help give them a better chance to survive. They would come to the ICU wards daily to do echocardiogram rounds to help determine changing cardiac function and optimal fluid treatment.

In the open wards and step-down ward tents, there was often a family atmosphere. When patients were discharged (often with tears), they were cheered by all in the tent. As they left the hot zone, staff would come out of the tents to encourage, cheer, clap and ring cowbells.

Our days continued until 7PM, when we would give sign out rounds to the incoming night shift (bless their hearts for taking this tough shift), grab dinner, change out of scrubs, and be transported back to our rooms, usually by about 8PM or shortly after. Then it was time to shower, call our families, read on patients medically, pray, and try to sleep.

During the day, because of the many admissions and rapidly changing patient conditions, I tried to limit breaks to two or so, as the PPE doffing and donning procedures took time. For me, this meant limiting fluid intake (I am 65) and grabbing a protein/candy bar after a bathroom break. Most others ate more sensibly than that; the SP food was complete and delicious.

We tried to be Jesus to these patients, especially since they had no one else to be with them. We prayed over their beds before they came, prayed for them daily (with permission) while they were with us and prayed with them and with their families.

Three patients stand out among many notables. The first, Thomas (not his real name) did not want neuromuscular paralysis or sedation while on the ventilator. He did require sedation just briefly, as we had to exchange his endotracheal tube twice due to occlusion by thick secretions. Otherwise, he was wide awake and alert while intubated for several days, watching with interest our days of hustling about the tent. He survived to be extubated and is now at home recovering. The second patient was Stephen (not his real name) who came to the ICU on CPAP on the cusp of needing ventilation. He was on the CPAP for a couple of days before he required ventilation, and was always asking us to come and pray with him and for him. This we did, and after his condition further deteriorated on ventilation, he was transferred to Mount Sinai Hospital. He is alive as I write this two weeks later, and still being weaned slowly. The third, Jose, (not his real name) almost died from his illness and upon recovery, has accepted Christ as his Savior! Thank you, Jesus!

During my stay, there were many high points; the best having just been mentioned. The ICU, ward EMTs, nurses, NPs, CRNAs and doctors were fantastic. They taught me volumes. We had a spirit of unity, teamwork, and consultation in order to best treat our patients. God provided all of us to strengthen each other.

The SP staff including leadership, support, chaplains, and mechanical were exceptional. I had no idea how taxing and unrelenting the minute by minute waves of crises could be. They are all amazing examples of servanthood. Support and mechanical staff worked day and night during high winds, downpours and flooding to keep us warm, dry and supplied with power, oxygen, food, clothing, medications and spiritual encouragement. They supplied us with a wealth of PPE.

The New Yorkers have been so kind and appreciative. At 7PM each evening, crowds came to the edge of the field hospital to extend to us "Clap Because We Care" by cheering, clapping, and ringing bells. They have donated truckloads of food, warm clothing, and headwear to make PPE comfortable. They express gratitude in the streets. Some have even donated apartments for staff to stay in. The Mount Sinai Medical staff were a tremendous resource to us, especially Drs. Wang, Tsung, and Croft - always ready to help in any way in a moment's notice, by phone or in person. The families of patients gave us understanding and appreciation in very difficult circumstances. Companies like Adidas donated long socks to keep the high rubber boots from chafing our legs, and Delta Airlines donated flights to transport staff to and from NYC. God has blessed us with all of these.

Of course, there were times when our spirits sank and we struggled. It is so very hard to give our everything to patients only to have many of them die anyway. It is so very hard to deliver that news or news of worsening conditions to frightened families who are separated from somebody they love. It is so very hard to be encouraged by a patient's improvement only to have that improvement collapse into further sickness in a matter of hours or even minutes. At times, regional shortages of medication born of an overwhelmed medical system made treatment more difficult. But God always provided.

Toward the end of my three weeks, when volume, turnover, and severity of patients' illness seemed to dramatically increase, I found myself doubting my abilities, my calling, and at times even doubting God's presence. Each time when this happened, I found that God's goodness showed up in so many ways: an unexpected improvement, a word of encouragement from a fellow worker, a prayer with a chaplain, or hearing of the multitude of prayers from all of those back home and around the world lifted us up. There were times I stuffed my emotions in the ICU until I could weep alone in my room at night. Other times I could not hold back and the tears came while I was in the tent with them.

I am still processing what felt like an emotional and spiritual tsunami, but I have relearned these things:

That God is always present, or especially present, even when I don't feel it. For me, this has often been a time when I am trying to do everything on my own, with my own "power". He reminds me of my complete dependence on Him. He tells me that He is enough. That the prayers of others are so powerful and important. Nothing was accomplished in Central Park without the sustaining prayers of the staff and believers around the world.

That God is so good. I have heard "God not only calls the equipped, but He equips the called." I felt fearful, anxious and alone when I came to NYC. I felt inadequate to contribute in a meaningful way. God showed me that what was important was my faith in and reliance on Him. He provided for these patients through our whole team, all the while blessing us with His goodness. I did not come to God in strength and righteousness except for that which He gives me in grace through the blood of Jesus. He stoops down to meet me, daily, in my brokenness. I am not the mover here or anywhere else. I am the one who is moved, and I am an avenue of His love and His power. "He gives strength to the weary and increases the power of the weak." Isaiah 40:29 (NIV). All praise to Him!

Final thoughts (Natalie Evans):

This project was born out of a desire to "record" this historical time in our world. I journaled during my time in Italy and wished to record my thoughts for my grandchildren someday. As I began typing my notes, I knew God was leading me to ask certain coworkers if they would consider adding their perspectives as well. I'm so glad they generously shared their experiences.

All the above medical personnel, I had personally worked with except for Dr. Michael Post. His synopsis of his time in New York City really resonated with me and I asked him, too, if he would be interested in "preserving" his story in this format. I am immensely grateful to everyone who shared! If time had allowed, I wish I could have gotten everyone's story!

I'd like to repeat Dr. Post's shared scripture and sentiment above, because it really expressed how I felt about this deployment:

"He gives strength to the weary and
increases the power of the weak."
Isaiah 40:29 (NIV)

"All praise to Him!"

References

Devine, A. (1911). Recollection. In *The Catholic Encyclopedia.* New York: Robert Appleton Company. Retrieved from: http://www.newadvent.org/cathen/12676b.htm

Muyskens, D. (2006). *Forty days to a closer walk with God: The practice of centering prayer.* Upper Room Books.

Ross-Gotta, L. (2001). To be virgin. In *Watch for the light: Readings for advent and Christmas (pp.96-97).* Plough Publishing House.

This is a simple journaling during a world crises. I am a simple person from a simple background, whom God has graciously done amazing things in my life. I'm a little girl from West Virginia, who moved to Florida. I'm a young bride. I'm a new mom from 25 to 35. I'm a "Mimi" at 50. And I'm a disaster response team member beginning at 52, who believes God gives strength to the weak. All praise to Him!

I am deeply grateful for the doctors, nurses and medical technologists who shared their contributions to this project. And I am grateful to all my coworkers in the faith!

Thank you!

Natalie Evans